How Successful Business People
Put the Old Rules Out to Pasture

Beau Fraser, David Bernstein,
and Bill Schwab

from The Gate Worldwide

 HYPERION

New York

Library of Congress Cataloging-in-Publication Data

Fraser, Beau.
  Death to all sacred cows / Beau Fraser, David Bernstein, and Bill Schwab.
    p. cm.
  ISBN 978-1-4013-0331-0
  1. Management—Philosophy. 2. Corporate culture. 3. Management—
Humor. 4. Corporate culture—Humor. 5. Business—Humor.
I. Bernstein, David, 1962– II. Schwab, Bill. III. Title.
  HD31.F718 2008
  658—dc22   2007012217

Hyperion books are available at special quantity discounts to use as premiums
or for special programs, including corporate training. For details contact
Michael Rentas, Proprietary Markets, Hyperion,
77 West 66th Street, 12th floor, New York, New York 10023,
or call 212-456-0133.

FIRST EDITION

1   3   5   7   9   10   8   6   4   2

BEAU FRASER:

To my father, who gave me a sense of humor.

To my mother, who taught me how to think.

To my sister, who teaches me to have a heart,

and to Kelly and Mara, who make me smile.

DAVID BERNSTEIN:

To the entire Bernstein family.

Especially my vegetarian wife, Peggy,

and our two carnivores, Zack and Kyra.

BILL SCHWAB:

To my father.

To my 2nd, 5th, and 7th grade English teacher,

who coincidentally is my mother,

and to Mary Sue and our children.

Contents

SECTION III (carcass)

Death To All Sacred Cows

SECTION I

(calf)

Introduction

In the Rigveda, one of the four most holy Hindu texts and the oldest of all religious books, it is written that "Cows are sacred." Man, if we had a nickel for every time we started a sentence with "In the Rigveda," we would be very wealthy guys. As it is, only one of us is wealthy and that's because his uncle invented Silly String.

At this juncture we feel it prudent to point out that Silly String was actually invented by Julius Sämann (who also invented pine tree–shaped air fresheners). Mr. Sämann is not related to any one of us (as far as we know). We admit this because it's important to establish a sense of trust between the author and the reader. Also you could have Googled Silly String and busted us anyway.

The important thing to remember here is not so much that we're liars, but that Sacred Cows have been roaming among us since around 1,700 BC. And, as George Foreman has proved time and time again, old things die hard.

So, what is a Sacred Cow? Or, as they say in Grenoble, *Qu'est-ce que c'est une Vache Sacré?* (We can't wait to see how they treat those last two sentences when they translate this book into French.) In the Hindu tradition, the Sacred Cow is an honored figure that represents the bounty of the earth, a mother's love, and the sanctity of life. In the world of commerce, the Sacred

Cow is a saying, motto, or aphorism about how business should be conducted that is widely assumed to be unassailably true.

This book is not about Hinduism, Indian Sacred Cows, fat boxers, or Swiss novelty inventors. This is a book about business. And the Sacred Cows to which we refer do not wander through the Indus Valley munching on subcontinental grasses and grains. The Sacred Cows that we plan on killing are pithy edicts repeated and sanctified and followed blindly by employees and management throughout the world.

They're a set of words, rules, or actions that businesspeople believe in primarily because businesspeople have always believed in them, so why stop now? These Cows have been passed down from generation to generation like creepy family heirlooms that ought to embarrass you but in which you take tremendous albeit incomprehensible pride. You know, like that picture of your great-grandfather dressed as a hula dancer. That shouldn't be on the mantelpiece. Who cares if he was a Navy captain crossing the equator for the first time? That photo should be kept in a dank, dark vault somewhere only to be used in extreme cases of blackmail.

The Sacred Cows of the business world—those phrases that everyone believes in without really bothering to analyze—all have worthwhile elements. At some point they made a lot of sense and had real value. Even though they have outlived their usefulness, they stubbornly stay in place as businesses, companies, employees, competitions, and cultures evolve around them. As time passes, they become the one unchangeable business constant remaking everything else in their image. You end up adapting your business to suit a philosophy instead of adapting your philosophy to suit your business.

There's nothing wrong with developing a philosophy based on a careful study of prior successes. A crafty businessman will look at a functioning concern and say, "This works and it has these properties." But there's an important distinction to be made between that analysis and the assertion that "This works *because* it has these properties." Once you start believing in the inevitability of a perceived cause and effect, you're falling for a Sacred Cow and you could be getting yourself into trouble. McDonald's works *and* they sell revolting food. McDonald's doesn't work *because* they sell revolting food. If it did, then the old lady with the glass eye who operates the roach coach in front of our office would be a billionaire.

These constraining thoughts are usually simple and cogent. They have to be plausible to stick around for so many years. After all, crazy doesn't last too long—just look at Mike Tyson. And, while we're mentioning famous heavyweights, why was Archie Moore called "The Ole Mongoose"? That's a weird nickname. Maybe you could look into it while you're Googling Silly String.

When we talk about Sacred Cows, we're talking about many of the fundamental tenets of commerce. A classic Sacred Cow of the ilk which we plan on destroying is "The Customer Is Always Right." Who in their right minds would take issue with that statement? Well, we would. And we did—you'll read about it in a few chapters.

The Customer Is Always Right is one of those archetypal catchphrases that companies latch on to and won't let go of, like a Rottweiler with a duckling clamped in its jaws. Someone in upper management announces at a board meeting that from now on their company will be dedicated to the principle that The Customer Is Always Right. And that'll be that. No one will argue. Everyone will fall into line. And the driving force behind that business will be a shallow platitude that looks good in a mission statement.

Sometimes this fervent adherence to corporate philosophy will lead to great success. There are plenty of shops out there that treat the Customer as if he or she is Always Right, and they thrive because of it. But it's the blindness and lack of healthy skepticism that Sacred Cows engender that lead to trouble. Sometimes they're right. But if you follow them without reason or flexibility, you'll never know when they're not right for a particular business transaction, product line, or situation.

Sometimes desperately servicing the primacy of the Customer can lead to a company's demise. Sometimes treating the Customer as if he or she is totally clueless is your surest route to victory. You may not believe us now, but you will once you have read this book. You may also want your money back—but that's between you and your bookstore.

We have assembled a list of some of the most widespread and beloved Sacred Cows of business. We have piled these Cows into a metaphoric killing floor in a theoretical cattle farm that is hypothetically in Montana (but definitely within 300 miles of Canada). In the ensuing pages we will wander among these lowing, ignorant beasts, striking vicious blows to their necks and shoulders with giant, razor-sharp medieval flails. We take no joy in this bloody, noisy, bone-and-cartilage-spewing slaughter. We do it as a service to humanity. Also, we got a large advance on the book, and if we don't write it, Hyperion will sue us.

The purpose of this book is not to replace old, stale Sacred Cows with newer, fresher ones. We're not going to make you watch us murder The Customer Is Always Right just to supplant it with The Customer Must Wear Toe Socks. That would defeat our purpose. It would also be insane. Our goal is to point out the inefficacy of slavishly conforming to any preconceived notions about how businesses should be run.

We will show you examples of companies and individuals who have failed because they believed too fiercely, unbendingly, and completely in a variety of Sacred Cows. We will also show you examples of companies and individuals who have succeeded because they flouted conventional wisdom and violated these revered principles. We will show you how to spot Sacred Cows and how best to avoid them in the future. We will point out burgeoning business philosophies that run the risk of turning into Sacred Cows if we're not careful. We will also make a lot of bizarre references, odd jokes, and discomfiting asides designed to amuse, bemuse, and tickle the fancy. If you favor an untickled fancy, then perhaps this book is not for you. In any event, we have a job to do. And, if we're going to undo 4,000 years of engrained behavior, we had better get started.

How To Spot
A Sacred Cow

How do you spot a Sacred Cow? It's easy. Sneak up on one while she's sleeping and carefully paint a spot on her side.

That was a classic example of perfectly crafted comedy. We set up the expectation of revealing how one could identify a Sacred Cow and then we replaced that expectation with an entirely unexpected result—how to paint a spot on a cow—making a play on the word "spot" in the process. There's just one problem with this brilliantly structured joke: It's not funny.

And, in that regard, our lame attempt at humor is a lot like the herds of Sacred Cows out there. They make sense, but they don't work. And, just like spotting a lousy comedian, picking out the Sacred Cows is pretty simple once you know what to look for.

Loud, flashy ties and sport coats with the sleeves rolled up are sure signs that the comedian is going to suck. Also, if they yell a lot right off the bat, they're probably trying to cover up the fact that anything they say at a normal volume won't elicit laughs.

Phrases like "Yes, but . . . ," "I'm going to level with you . . . ," and "We can't do it that way, let's just . . ." are sure signs that you're about to hear a Sacred Cow. They can be bold mottoes etched in gold or quaint aphorisms stitched in yarn. They can be old technologies, tired products, rigid processes, dated services, or complacent management. They are the living embodiment of "we don't do things that way here." Sacred Cows survive by keeping everything the same.

Sacred Cows are a lot like thoroughbred horses in that both are the result of years of selective breeding. Virtually all thoroughbreds alive are descended from one of three stallions: the Darley Arabian, the Godolphin Arabian, and the Byerly Turk. All three were imported to England and bred to local mares. A great-great-grandson of the Darley Arabian, Eclipse, became an undefeated champion and sired 344 future winners. His perfect genes were in such demand that today 95% of all thoroughbreds are his heirs.

What does this have to do with Sacred Cows? Almost nothing. Except for the fact that these divine bovines have similarly identifiable bloodlines. They are usually sired by corporate management. Some cigar smoker with a comb-over demands to know, "Well . . . what's the formula?" and another Sacred Cow is born. These high-stepping philosophical fillies have descended from boardroom to boardroom and manager to manager over the ages.

The people who perpetuate these creative handcuffs have a lot in common and can easily be identified as well. By and large, they tend to be negative. They seem to think that they're not contributing if they're not criticizing. When asked for an opinion, it's invariably depressing and pessimistic. For these people it's much easier to raise objections than to embrace something new and different—even if that new and different thing might lead to greatness.

They usually can't tell you why they're shooting down your idea, although there's some vague reference to "that not working back in '03." When you innocently inquire whether that was 1503 or 1603, they look at you like you just peed in the clam dip.

Assuming that you didn't just pee in the clam dip, their whole attitude is bitter, unnecessary, and divisive.

Even when citing previous failures as a reason not to try something new, they don't bother drawing helpful conclusions from those failures. It's just "That didn't work, move on." Sometimes a nuanced understanding of past disasters helps lead to future achievements. But these Sacred Cow Midwives aren't interested in learning and changing—they just want to maintain the status quo. That's the whole raison d'être of the Sacred Cow to begin with—it just wants to keep on keeping on.

How many times did the Wright Brothers fail before they succeeded? We have no idea, and we all have carpal tunnel syndrome so we don't want to check the Internet. It was a lot, though, right? Man Cannot Fly was a pretty unassailable Sacred Cow. It was based on history, physics, and common sense. If the Wright Brothers had been working for the goofball who runs your marketing department, they might have been forced to give up after their first crash. If they'd been working for us, maybe we would have waited until their tenth crash before pulling the plug. But they were following their own vision and they knew it would work. All the logic and gravity and bloody head wounds didn't diminish their conviction. And they did away with that Sacred Cow forever. Now we're dealing with a much more entrenched Sacred Cow: Man Cannot Fly Coach But Business Class Is Criminally Overpriced. As soon as someone kills that one, we'll travel overseas again.

Sacred Cows
Down Through The Ages

battle

The year is 197 BC. Rubik has just invented his Cube and short skirts are in. No. Wait. The Macedonian army is kicking the pants off the Romans. That's right. The Romans have run roughshod over most of the known world. But now they're getting whacked by these pesky Macedonians.

A major battle is about to begin. Beer vendors and pretzel salesmen ply their wares. Don Knotts stretches his hamstrings and heads for the main tent at *Circus of the Stars*. Hold it. We're getting mixed up again.

The Macedonian army stands in their conventional fighting pattern, shield-to-shield, sixteen men deep. This is how they always fight. So far, they have always won.

The Roman army is about to meet them in combat in the same traditional array, and they're about to lose again. All that empire building right down the toilet (or, in this case, right down the public latrine cleansed with aqueduct water).

Suddenly a Roman tribune has an idea. What if, instead of fighting the Macedonians the "right" way—marching forward until they're face-to-face and then engaging—what if they fight them the "wrong" way? What if they attack from behind, surprising them and making it impossible to defend themselves with their huge, unwieldy shields and their cumbersome twenty-one-foot spears?

There are two things you can say about Romans: 1) they cheat at soccer, and 2) they hate hypothetical questions. So the tribune immediately puts his query into practice. They sneak behind the Macedonians and attack their rear, if you will. The outnumbered Romans kill over a third of the Macedonian army, win the war, and add another massive chunk to their empire.

What does any of this have to do with Sacred Cows? Why, it's as plain as the nose on the back of your hand. The operative Sacred Cow here was Always Fight Facing Your Enemy. The Macedonians believed in it, and it led to many great successes. But they believed in it too much and were unable to adapt or adjust when they came across an enemy who wasn't so tied to the same philosophy of war.

With one bold move, the Romans killed that Sacred Cow and a whole lot of Macedonians as well. They went on to rule the world, and Rome is still a great place to visit. Macedonia, on the other hand, is now a small and all-but-forgotten republic in Southeastern Europe (no offense to our many Macedonian fans currently reading this book in Circassian at the Skopje bookstore on the corner of Third and Jakupica).

cattle

Around 1,700 years later there was another example of a civilization sliding into obsolescence due to their steadfast refusal to alter their belief in a Sacred Cow. In this case, the Sacred Cow was Norse Greenlanders Eat Meat. And the people who paid the heavy price for not budging from this theory were the Norse

Greenlanders. In case you're not up-to-date on your Arctic demographics, there are no more Norse Greenlanders.

Erik the Red—a charming, exiled, convicted murderer—led a watery convoy of twenty-five ships filled with Norsemen and Norsewomen around 985 AD. He landed on a northern isle, liked the fertile soil and freshwater lakes he found there, so he named the place Greenland and decided to stay.

For around 500 years the colony prospered. They built farms, churches, and civic halls—for all we know they even built discos and mini-malls. But in the sixteenth century when a German ship landed on Greenland to escape an ice storm, they discovered . . . nothing. The farms, churches, and halls were abandoned and decaying. There wasn't a single Norse Greenlander left.

So, what happened to them all? Were they characters in some kind of creepy M. Night Shyamalan movie? Were they wintering in Boca Raton? Or did they fall victim to yet another deleterious Sacred Cow?

The truth is that no one really knows for sure. There's very little forensic evidence left to tell us anything definitive about this mysteriously evaporated culture. So, yes, it's possible that they were all extras in a weird movie where the villagers are really aliens and they are suddenly recalled to the mother ship. And, sure, there's a chance that they all moved to Florida. But anthropologists and social historians have another slightly more plausible explanation.

The Norse Greenlanders were meat eaters. They raised cattle and sheep, which were the mainstays of their diet. One of the reasons that Erik the Red called Greenland Greenland was that he knew it would attract settlers. They'd focus on the word "green," think it would be a great place for their sheep and cattle to graze, and they'd move there in a flash.

And that's just what happened. For years the Norse Greenlanders raised their livestock and coexisted with the native Inuit population. During the fourteenth and fifteenth centuries, however, there was a mini ice age in the Northern Hemisphere and the grasslands started dying out. The Norse Greenlanders couldn't feed their cattle and sheep, so the animals started dying out as well.

Something radical needed to be done. They had to change the way they lived. But the rigid structure of their society didn't allow for full-scale paradigm adjustment. They had an example of a way to survive right in front of their faces. The Inuit culture revolved around fishing. They ate fish, burned fish oil, and traded fish for hundreds of years—that's how they thrived. But the Norse Greenlanders were cow people: They ate cows, and they slavishly followed Sacred Cows. They saw a functioning model of how to survive Greenland's changing climate, but they couldn't or wouldn't adapt to it.

There is no direct archaeological evidence that suggests that the Norsemen ever ate any fish. Even when their crops were killed and they were reduced to eating the newborn calves right down to the hooves (which, by the way, are delicious in a spicy red sauce). When the calves were gone, they ate their household pets (also nice in a fiery *marinara* or *puttanesca*).

The most likely fate that befell the Norse Greenlanders was that the entire settlement died of starvation. The Inuits, meanwhile, continue to prosper on Greenland. And fishing is still the island's primary source of income.

In many ways, the demise of the Norse Greenlanders is a perfect metaphor for the dangers of the Sacred Cow. They stuck with what had made them successful, ignoring a changing environment, until the very philosophy that used to work for them ended up wiping them out.

prattle

We'll level with you: We called this section "prattle" because it rhymes with "battle" and "cattle." The following example has nothing to do with Ancient Rome, Norse Greenland, or childish baby talk. Although it is about Hollywood, so perhaps "prattle" isn't such a misleading title after all.

Just as there were Sacred Cows that dictated the ways they fought in the classical world and ate in the Arctic, there are Sacred Cows that rule the making of movies too. Here are three industry-wide, generally accepted Hollywood Sacred Cows about how to craft a hugely successful film: Blockbusters Can't Be Longer Than Two Hours, Blockbusters Can't Have Sad Endings, Blockbusters Shouldn't Be About Real Historical Events Because Everyone Knows The Ending.

Okay. So, there are your rules—go make your movie. If you followed these rules you could have made *ET*, *Men in Black*, *Wedding Crashers*, and *Finding Nemo*. And, if you have made all those movies, please give us a call because we need a loan to purchase Guam.

There is one blockbuster, however, that you couldn't have made if you followed these Sacred Cows. And this is the block-bustiest of all blockbusters.

In 1997 James Cameron made a little film about a doomed ocean liner. The movie lasted over three hours. Almost everyone in it dies. The entire audience knew before sitting down that the boat was going to sink. So even the briefest description of the film clearly shows that it rejected three inviolate precepts of moviemaking.

Regardless of all that, however, *Titanic* has grossed almost two billion dollars worldwide. Do you realize how much money that is? That's two billion dollars. Two billion dollars! That's a lot of Silly String.

We don't know why this movie was so staggeringly successful. Frankly, we don't even like it. It's maudlin, trite, and we wanted to fast-forward to the boat sinking and then leave as soon as it sank. But the point is it worked. You don't have to understand why it worked to appreciate the fact that sometimes it pays to kill a Sacred Cow.

Ultimately movies and armies and eating habits all fall under the same forces as products in the marketplace. The rules governing them are based on the past. We can ascertain what worked in the past and presume it may work in the future, but we can never *know* what will work in the future. Educated guesses are fine and usually lead to success. But that's really all these Sacred Cows are: They're educated guesses hallowed and sanctified over years of use. Employ them to your advantage. But it's best to be flexible enough to jettison them when they no longer suit your needs.

If James Cameron hadn't had the gumption to break those Hollywood rules, he never would have made the biggest grossing movie of all time. Instead he would have had to find a way to make-do with the paltry profits from his other bombs like *Aliens*, *Terminator*, and *Terminator II*. Hey, maybe we should call Cameron for the Guam loan . . .

Why Sacred Cows Deserve To Die

We are not philosophers, theoreticians, or brilliant academics. Frankly, we're not even that smart. One of us didn't break 900 on his SATs. Although, in his defense, not knowing the word "Lilliputian" is more a reflection of not having read *Gulliver's Travels* than a lack of intellectual aptitude. Anyway, we all know those tests are culturally biased; we just can't figure out which culture is catching all the breaks. Be that as it may, we have pooled our meager brainpower and come up with a reason for killing Sacred Cows that even geniuses like Copernicus, Marie Curie, and Wayne Newton have never thought of.

Sacred Cows deserve to die because, by killing them, you can save time, money, and lives. Perhaps you're thinking that, in business, lives aren't frequently at risk. At first blush this is true. But waiting for the second blush has bought us a fishing shack on the Delaware and a slightly used Jet Ski. These Sacred Cows of business can kill. Because if you keep wasting time and money, you'll be broke in no time. And, if you're broke, your husband or wife might leave, taking the house and the kids but not the mangy, farting dog. And, at that point, what have you got left to live for? QED, baby.

Blindly following firmly established rules can be a comfort for a while. But ending up poor, homeless, lonely, and smelly is nobody's version of a happy ending. It's essential to spot the kinds of thoughts, sayings, and directives that create tunnel vision and stymie growth. Once spotted, they need to be stamped out.

For years, we labored under the assumption that cows cannot walk backward. We thought that when they wanted to return to the barn, they had to make wide, cumbersome U-turns, like eighteen-wheelers trying to do doughnuts in a 7-Eleven parking lot. Looking back, we have no idea why we believed this piffle. Perhaps as children we were lied to by a drunken dairy farmer. Anyway, of course cows can go backward. Which shouldn't surprise us, after all, because Sacred Cows go backward all the time. The majority of these business aphorisms revolve around how great things used to be and how much better it all was then than it is now. In that regard, studying these sayings is a lot like talking to your great-uncle Charlie. We have no idea why almost freezing to death in the Hürtgen Forest should be preferable to playing skeeball at Chuck E. Cheese's, but Uncle Charlie certainly seems to think it is.

Businesses that only look to the past to guide their futures can be doomed to failure. In a rapidly changing world, anything dated tends to be dangerous. Especially teenagers. Don't ever date teenagers if you want to succeed on a management level. Unless you're a Doogie Howser-esque teenage executive—in which case, knock yourself out.

If the world was a stagnant, predictable place, then steadfast rules would be okay. They would guide us and keep everyone honest. But the world in which we live changes constantly. One day infants are supposed to sleep on their sides. The next day they tell you that babies have to sleep on their backs. And the next day they tell you that Britney Spears's career is over. It's hard to keep up. Anything more rigid than a guideline should be immediately second-guessed.

If we don't question why we do things the way we do, we'll never be able to do them better. If we resist new approaches, we'll be stuck with more of the same all the time. And if all your decisions are based on Sacred Cows, which are rooted in the past, then your business will never have a chance to grow. You'll end up like Britney Spears—probably without the embarrassing Internet photos or the millions in the bank—but you'll be just as obsolete.

Companies, like shooting ranges and the suburbs, have targets. They have goals. For most enterprises, the primary goal is to beat the competition—whoever is one or two rungs ahead on the giant, swaying ladder of business. But what if you redefined "competition"? What if, instead of the store across the street, you thought of your competition as the things that prevent you from succeeding?

If you sell beanbags and you're not selling as many as you'd like, what's holding you back? Is it really the beanbag wholesaler down on Route 8? Or is it the myriad stifling rules and instructions you're operating under? If you want to beat that Route 8 guy with his fancy silk upholstery filled with mungs and chickpeas and other genera of exotic *Fabaceae*, then you have to stop following those Sacred Cows and start making a new plan.

Maybe you should reinvent yourself as the organic beanbag shop. Maybe your beanbags should feature cooked beans so that, in times of famine, your comfy chairs will provide a readily available food source. Maybe you should get rid of the bags altogether and just sell beans, or lose the beans and just sell bags. We don't know. If we did, we'd be the beanbag guys instead of the Sacred Cow guys. The point is, in order to prepare for the future you need to unchain yourself from the strictures of the past. Let the past help and inform you; just don't let it hold you back.

You don't have any control over the outside world unless you're some kind of wizard or warlock (we don't know the difference, but we know enough not to mess with either one). You do, however, have control over your world. If you're not number one or number two in your field, then you'll need to kill some Sacred Cows to get noticed and get ahead. If you are number one or number two, then you'll need to kill some Sacred Cows to stay where you are and keep the other guys from catching you. And, if you're a warlock or a wizard, you can do whatever you want as long as you don't turn us into frogs, pillars of salt, or circus freaks. We thank you in advance.

Ten Phrases That Immediately Precede
The Announcement Of A Sacred Cow

1. I'm just spitballing here, but . . .
2. My great-grandfather made a killing by always . . .
3. Instincts, shminstincts! Let's just . . .
4. It's time to think outside the box. Birnbaum, what have you got?
5. Ooh, that sounds a little too risky—how about if we just . . .
6. The voice of God came to me in a dream and told me to . . .
7. Hey, you know what worked at my last job?
8. I don't care how passionately you believe in it, Jenkins, what we're actually going to do is . . .
9. There's only one way to get this company on its feet again and that's to . . .
10. Let's just listen to what these really expensive consultants I hired have to say . . .

Ten Things To Say Immediately After
The Announcement Of A Sacred Cow

1. That wasn't spitballing, that was spitting. Here's a han-kie.
2. If your great-grandfather was so smart, how come he's so dead?
3. You need to spend less time rhyming and more time dig-ging your way out of corporate debt.
4. Thinking outside the box is just another way of saying you're an idiot. Let's just think of something good and not worry so much about geometry. And my name's not Birnbaum.
5. Nothing's too risky to try if there's thought and passion behind it.
6. I stand corrected. Listening to the voices in your head is too risky. Please have a lobotomy.
7. If that worked so well at your last job, how come you're not at your last job anymore?
8. Passion shouldn't be dismissed out of hand. My name's not Jenkins either.
9. There are thousand ways to get this company on its feet again, and they all begin with getting rid of you.
10. Overpaid consultants should have their own ring in hell, but the Devil can't afford to hire them to consult on what that ring should be like.

Death To All Sacred Cows

SECTION II

(cows)

Always Trust
Your Research

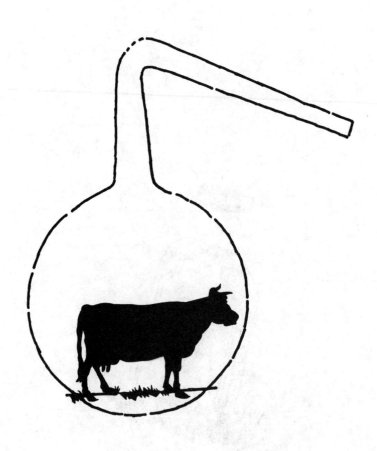

"Always Trust Your Research" is an edict by which businesses have been swearing ever since businesses first began to swear (this usually happens during the summer of their twelfth year—thirteen if they're late bloomers). But what does "Trusting Your Research" really mean? And, for that matter, what does "Research" really mean?

"Research": from the Medieval French *recerche* (1577) meaning "the act of searching closely." Do we speak French? No. Do we know anything about France, history, or etymology? No. You know how we knew all that stuff? Because we did the research. We did the research on research.

Research is what you have to get done before anyone can do anything. Without research you're just guessing. Without research you're just hoping. Without research you're nothing, let's face it. Testing. Focus groups. Polls. Questionnaires. Internet surveys. It's all part of the multiheaded monster called research.

Our company isn't called The Gate because it sounds good when sung out loud in the shower. That's just a happy accident. The name "The Gate" was tested. It was researched. The research said, "Go ahead and call your company The Gate." And we have prospered. That's not to say we wouldn't have prospered if our company was called Hot Fudge in a Bag. But our company isn't called Hot Fudge in a Bag. Because, just as they taught us in business school, we Trusted Our Research.

Always Trust Your Research. Sounds like a sound philosophy, doesn't it? But don't fall in love with this Sacred Cow, because it's time for it to die. In this chapter we will prove beyond a shadow of a doubt that Always Trusting Your Research is simply not a sound business philosophy. And our supporting evidence is so strong, that we will prove this over three hundred yards beyond a shadow of a doubt—and that's tough to do even with today's newfangled titanium drivers.

iced tea

In China, tea is big. This is, like, the mother of all truisms. There's over a billion Chinese and almost all of them drink tea. So, in 1999, when the Beihua Beverage Company had the bright idea of introducing iced tea to China, it seemed like a no-brainer. In the business world, however, there's no such thing as a no-brainer. At some point, everyone runs everything past someone with some brains. And usually that's when the trouble starts.

Soon after the iced tea idea had been floated, Liu Qiang, the Beihua Beverage Company's research director, decided to do what he did best—research. He organized taste tests and conducted market studies to make sure that selling iced tea to the Chinese really was a good idea.

His research was conclusive. The Chinese didn't want iced tea. Over 60% of research subjects rejected Beihua's product. Consequently the company immediately abandoned the development of iced tea and forgot about the whole thing.

The next year, however, another beverage company, Xu Ri

Sheng, launched their own iced tea into the Chinese market. And guess what? It was a huge success.

The folks back at Beihua scratched their collective heads. Where had they gone wrong? Their research had been clear. Iced tea shouldn't have worked in China. But it did.

So, Liu Qiang—quite possibly worried about his job and whatever bonus was supposed to have been coming his way—took another look at the research to try to solve the mystery. And it wasn't much of a mystery. Qiang realized that their research had been conducted in the middle of winter. Testing subjects came in out of the cold and weren't given time to warm up. Naturally, when they were offered freezing cold glasses of iced tea, they politely declined.

Research is good. Research is important. But research is numbers and graphs and charts. Numbers, graphs, and charts will never be as intuitive as a clever person with good instincts. Research may give us some answers. But we shouldn't rely on research to give us all the answers.

When you first read that a company was going to introduce iced tea into the Chinese market, what was your reaction? Ours was "I can't believe the Chinese didn't already have iced tea." And our next reaction was "Wow, that's a brilliant and incredibly obvious idea that is going to make someone very, very rich." When an idea feels that right, you can't just abandon it because of some research statistics. Sometimes you have to let common sense overwhelm the tyranny of the Sacred Cow.

ice-t

And speaking of common sense, how about that gangsta rap? We love it! It's loud, it rhymes, and it spells gangsta with an "a" instead of an "er" which is creative and insouciant. But what, we're sure you're asking, does gangsta rap have to do with research, Sacred Cows, the business world, or anything else for that matter?

We'll tell you.

Tracy Marrow, better known as Ice-T, the rapper/actor/entrepreneur, is one of the unofficial founders of gangsta rap. Ice-T is also a stone-cold killer . . . of Sacred Cows. Actually he just killed one . . . and he did it by accident . . . and he probably doesn't even know he did it . . . but it still counts.

Tracy was born in New Jersey, but he grew up in South Central Los Angeles where—according to documented reports, industry insiders, and every time Ice-T opens his mouth—he became a member of the Crips. While focusing his energies in bandana-fueled drug deals and random gang activity, Tracy/Ice was also dabbling in making music.

In 1987 he stopped dabbling and started taking music seriously. He signed a deal with a major label, Sire Records, and he released his debut album *Rhyme Pays*. And it did pay. *Rhyme Pays*, a collection of mainly party-themed songs, went gold. But Ice-T didn't want to just churn out lame party tunes. He wanted to make music that reflected the reality of what was going on in the streets—the gangbanging and violence that was going on in the streets, not so much the spirited games of roller hockey. Sire Records wanted to make music that would get on the radio and move lots of units. Ice-T wanted to make music with lyrics that rhymed with "snitch," "bigger," and "truck." Sire Records wouldn't go for it.

Why was Sire Records (and, in fact, all the major labels at that time) so opposed to releasing the kind of hard-core music that Ice-T wanted to develop? You guessed it—research.

All the significant research of the day pointed to one obvious fact: radio stations would not play music that contained graphic language and obvious references to violence and obscenity. Research also clearly stated that, without radio play, records don't sell. That's why record companies pay radio stations to play their music (allegedly). So that constant repetition will convince a gullible audience to spend money on music they wouldn't even listen to if the radio stations hadn't been colluding with the record companies to begin with (allegedly).

So here's Tracy Marrow aka Ice-T, and he's faced with a quandary. Does he take the easy money and make more party albums for Sire Records? Or does he ignore the market research and make raw and offensive albums that won't get any radio play?

For most people, this would have been a hard decision. But once you've rhymed "assistance" with "social persistence," the world is pretty much your oyster. So Ice-T left Sire Records, started his own label, and began to release the kind of brutal, violent music for which he became so well known and which is responsible for it being impossible to spend more than five minutes in a car with our receptionist's nephew Eric.

And the research was right. He didn't get much radio play. But the research was wrong. Because, even without radio play, Ice-T albums started flying off the shelves. And his success paved the way for other hard-core rap groups like N.W.A to do the same. You didn't hear Ice-T's "O.G." or N.W.A's "Straight Outta Compton" on the radio. But you heard them blasting out of everyone's car (especially Eric's).

Ice-T changed the way the music business operates. His album sales were the object lesson that taught record executives not to "Always Trust Their Research." And, by killing that one Sacred Cow, Ice-T helped transform an industry. These days almost every major label has a whole division dedicated to developing and selling rap acts, regardless of the radio-friendliness of their lyrics.

At the end of the day, research will answer the questions it is asked. If you ask the wrong questions in the wrong way, don't blame the research when someone else ends up selling gangsta rap in the suburbs or iced tea to the Chinese.

It's Okay To Put Up With Jerks, If They're Talented

We'll let you in on a little secret: In the past, we have been called jerks. It only happened once—we got caught cheating at Battleship in sixth grade—but it happened and we'll be damned if we're going to lie about it. That experience taught us two valuable lessons: 1) Try not to be a jerk, and 2) Never position your destroyer next to your PT boat. There are a lot of folks out there, however, who have not learned these lessons. You still hear horror stories about people putting their destroyers in the stupidest places. And you hear horror stories about jerks in business too.

What exactly is a jerk at work (aside from a charming semi-rhyme)? They're easy to spot when they're super-obvious. You've got Leona Helmsley clawing at her underlings with razor-sharp old-lady talons. You've got Donald Trump unctuously firing the normally coiffed in front of millions. And you've got Simon Cowell viciously berating far more talented people while never acknowledging that his hairdo may be even more preposterous than Donald Trump's. But jerks abound in all shapes, sizes, and personality profiles.

At one company where the corporate vibe is gung-ho, in-your-face aggressiveness, a jerk may have to go a country mile to stand out. At another, more laid-back workplace, maybe the jerk's just the lady who keeps eating other people's apple turnovers (even though we label them clearly). The bottom line is: If you're always apologizing for someone at work, then that person is probably a jerk. And if everyone's always apologizing for you—guess what?—you're the jerk (congratulations).

Everyone has a defense for these people. "You don't understand him." "She's under a lot of pressure." "Don't take offense—it's just his way." "She didn't mean to shatter your collection of antique glass paperweights." And they're always defended for the same reason: They're successful.

When unproductive office slackers call the receptionist Sugar Pants, they get fired. When the hotshot ad exec who just landed the major soft drink account calls the receptionist Sugar Pants, everyone laughs. Even the receptionist laughs. But, then again, he laughs at everything.

The business world is like the real world—it's not fair. Sometimes nice guys finish last and obnoxious creeps get rewarded. When obnoxious creeps are perceived as contributing to a healthy bottom line, they get rewarded more than most.

Sometimes people feel that they have no choice but to put up with talented jerks. By all accounts, Ty Cobb was a world-class creep. He was a cruel thug who once went into the stands to beat up a heckler who had only two fingers. But he had a lifetime batting average of .366 and over 4,000 hits. Without him the Tigers could not have won. They felt that they had to put up with his racism and violent temper. In today's business world, overt racism would never be tolerated, but people put up with all kinds of other aberrant behavior in the name of talent and success. No one, however, is so talented or successful that they should be allowed to abuse others. No one should tolerate a foulmouthed, inappropriate boor just because he or she turns a profit or hustles singles into doubles (and we're not picking on Ty Cobb here. We also have a big problem with Pete Rose—but don't get us started).

The same logic that protects these egomaniacal jackasses can be used to get rid of them as well. Why didn't that hotshot ad exec get fired? Because he landed the soft drink account. But what's going to happen when, instead of insulting the reception-ist, he accidentally insults the soft drink president's wife? How valuable will he be then? And, sure, the guy's bringing in rev-enue to the company. But think of what he's doing to office morale and productivity. How hard is the rest of your staff working when they're constantly being abused by this guy? Is keeping him around really worth more than letting him go? Sometimes you have to look below the bottom line to find out what something's really costing you.

it guy

Michael Schrage is the codirector of the MIT Media Lab's eMarkets Initiative and a senior adviser to MIT's Securities Studies Program. We have no idea what that means, but he's very successful and a lot of people a lot smarter than us listen to him. He consults for a variety of mega-businesses, offering ad-vice on new product development and corporate transformation (among other subjects).

In a recent article in *CIO* magazine, Schrage mentioned that he is often asked for free business advice. He responds to these requests thusly: "The most cost-effective way to dramatically improve your IT organization's implementation of a new sys-tem, app, or upgrade is to make sure you fire the right person."

The "right person" that Schrage is talking about is our hypo-thetical successful jerk. He believes that all good managers know who this person is, but they keep coming up with reasons to keep him or her around because they're scared to lose a productive worker. But just because Jerk A is good at their job doesn't mean they should keep their job. Schrage says that sometimes firing Jerk A is essential not only because it strengthens office morale but also because it makes a clear statement about your corporate philosophy.

Schrage offers a personal anecdote to clarify this point. He was working for a Fortune 500 IT company once, consulting on how to improve collaboration between the technology and business units. He found the corporate culture there to be way too polite and nonconfrontational. So, he started pushing his philosophy about the importance of communication and confrontation. He pushed pretty hard.

The head of the company called Schrage into his office. He thanked Schrage for his time, his help, and his expertise but explained to him that the company was very proud of its "consensus culture." He also pointed out that Schrage's tone and attitude were unacceptable, and he politely informed him that his services were no longer required.

Granted, he was just a consultant. And, granted, he was just trying to help. But in that corporate environment Michael Schrage had, unwittingly and momentarily, turned into a jerk. And the jerk got fired—just as Schrage recommends. He certainly couldn't argue with that. And neither can we.

tv guy

This next charming tale can be corroborated by a variety of sources including the Internet, many entertainment industry periodicals, and our friend Andrew. Yes, someone we know and trust (more or less) has had firsthand interaction with Mr. Stephen Chao and survived—a little shaken, a little stirred, but a lot wiser for having glimpsed into the gaping maw of the Jerk At Work.

Almost every facet of Mr. Chao's curriculum vitae bellows out, "Beware!" First, he went to Harvard. Need we say more? (They rejected all three of us.) Next, after graduation he took a job as a reporter at the *National Enquirer*. To our knowledge, those jobs are usually forced on convicted felons as terms of their work-release programs. Then he had the temerity to go back to Harvard to get his MBA. And, finally, as if the inevitability of his jerkishness wasn't clear enough, he took a job working for Rupert Murdoch.

Our friend crossed paths with Mr. Chao when he was developing television shows for Fox TV. Andrew met with Chao to pitch him a few ideas. Instead of respectfully listening to the pitch and then rejecting it (like every other TV executive did), Mr. Chao spent the meeting figuring out who he and Andrew knew in common and then spreading salacious rumors about each of them. The fact that he was, in almost every instance, completely correct about the juicy tidbit(s), in no way ameliorated the inappropriate tenor of the meeting.

Andrew's disapproval, however, did not stop Stephen Chao from achieving success. He was smart, he was quick, and he was ambitious. Everyone tolerated his obnoxiousness because he got results. Pretty soon he became president of Fox TV and Fox News. His prurient tastes and flair for boorishness led to the development of such wonderful shows as *America's Most Wanted*, *Cops*, and *Studs*. It was almost as if Stephen Chao turned jerkiness into a cottage industry.

And then like Icarus, whom he surely knew about since he was a Classics major, he flew too close to the sun. At a top-level management conference attended by the likes of Rupert Murdoch and Dick Cheney, Stephen Chao hired a male stripper to perform. We think he was attempting to make some kind of point about freedom of speech. All he succeeded in doing, however, was to offend, insult, and infuriate everyone.

Rupert Murdoch finally reached the realization that no jerk is talented enough to be tolerated in the workplace. Stephen Chao was summarily fired. And, while he has resurfaced from time to time like a bad penny or a breaching whale, Mr. Chao's career was never the same. He never fulfilled his early promise and he failed to seamlessly transition from wunderkind to éminence gris. We hope that this fateful stripper conference finally taught him a valuable lesson about not being a jerk. Unfortunately for all of us, Dick Cheney must not have been paying attention.

The Gate Strikes Back:
Five Sacred Cows Of Advertising

1. "Always include the brand name in the headline."
—David Ogilvy

David Ogilvy was an advertising genius, an excellent chef, a lousy tobacco farmer, and a British spy. He wasn't, however, always right. Trumpeting the name of the product you're trying to sell is often an excellent strategy. But one of our favorite ad campaigns never said a word about anything. In 1990, a bevy of animal topiaries suddenly started appearing throughout Los Angeles. Yup, you read us right—these were large bushes trimmed to look like animals. No one knew why they were there. There was no signage, no ad copy, no brand name—nothing. But, little by little, word started seeping out that they were promoting a strange, new movie about to be released called *Edward Scissorhands*. Within a few days, everyone in the town that has seen it all was talking about something they'd never seen. The advance buzz on *Edward Scissorhands* helped launch the movie successfully, and it remains our favorite movie of all time about a boy with scissors for hands.

Focus On The Numbers,
And The Rest Will
Take Care Of Itself

Without wanting to wallow in the muddy pool of philosophy, we would like to pose an ontological query: What is business? Some might say that business is the machinery of daily life, the getting and spending that Wordsworth so eloquently disparaged. Some might say that business is the lifeblood of the international community. And some might say that we should shut up. Frankly, we're of the third opinion. Because, when it comes to business, there's no need for all the wordy hooha. At the end of the day, business is numbers.

What are numbers? (Man, we just can't avoid the big questions, can we?) Well, numbers are . . . um . . . heck, we all know what numbers are, right? They're your bottom line. Your net profit or your overhead totals. The numbers are what make it worthwhile to launch a new product or recall an old one. The numbers are your employees or your target demographic or your overstocked widgets or your understocked gizmos. (Note to self: Never understock gizmos—the public positively clamors for them.) The numbers are whatever drives your business when all the bells and whistles are stripped away.

Focusing on the numbers is the one part of business that anyone with a calculator, a slide rule, and/or one of those green plastic visors can do; it doesn't require nuance or subtlety. Perhaps that's the appeal that these numbers have for so many businesses—they reduce the risks of the human element. But without the human element, that ineffable quality that makes each person distinct and each company stand out, all businesses would just blend together into a homogenous swamp of commerce. (Another note to self: Charge more for using "ineffable" and "homogenous" in the same sentence.)

You can talk all you want about corporate culture and employee loyalty, but if the numbers don't add up, your business ain't working. So, it's tough to argue with that age-old Sacred Cow: "Focus On The Numbers And The Rest Will Take Care Of Itself." But we're nothing if not argumentative. Because great numbers are a byproduct of success, they're not the objective. Nobody that we know of is in the business of numbers. You can't sell 7 or lease out 362. However, you can sell high-quality lawn furniture or lease out attractively priced ocean-view villas. And, if you do a good job at this, great numbers will follow. Sometimes just Focusing On The Numbers can actually get you into trouble.

chainsaw

Maybe we're idiots, but we think there's something preternaturally pleasing about small household appliances. You can keep your magic acts, jugglers, and clowns (especially clowns—yikes). Toaster ovens, waffle-makers, and handheld mixing devices—these are the things that put smiles on our faces.

For over sixty years, the good folks at Sunbeam have agreed with us. Can openers, hair dryers, tea makers—that's what it's all about over at Sunbeam. Bread makers, curling irons, vaporizers—these people put toasty, melted sandwiches and rich, fruity smoothies within the grasp of anyone who can find a Wal-Mart.

It comes as no surprise to us that Sunbeam grew from its humble beginnings in post–World War II Chicago to become a billion-dollar international company. It comes as somewhat of a surprise, however, that the company ran into serious problems in the mid-'90s. Had people suddenly tired of lightweight irons, electric blankets, and outdoor grills? We don't know. But Sunbeam was hurting. Their stock was plummeting. Their numbers were low.

So Sunbeam did what many other flagging companies have done in similar circumstances: They called in an expert. Unfortunately for just about everybody involved, the expert they called in was "Chainsaw" Al Dunlap.

Chainsaw Al had gone to great lengths to earn his charming sobriquet by slicing away thousands of workers from the payrolls of a variety of companies that he had run. Dunlap's philosophy was that the only people who matter in a publicly held corporation are the shareholders. And the way to increase the net worth of the shareholders is by making ruthless budget cuts, layoffs, and plant closings. Al always focused on the numbers, and the rest always took care of itself.

His technique had been incredibly successful. In the four years before arriving at Sunbeam, he had earned over $100 million and was lauded as a genius by Wall Street. The day that his arrival at Sunbeam was announced, Sunbeam stock increased by 50%.

Once installed in his cushy office, Chainsaw Al went to work. Within four months, he had gotten rid of two-thirds of Sunbeam's plants and he had fired half of its employees. The stock went up. Chainsaw Al kept focusing on the numbers. He had earnings estimates to meet, and he would do whatever it took to meet or surpass them. And he did. For a while.

But within a few years it became clear that Al was putting

Sunbeam in an untenable position. In his desperate effort to make the numbers make sense, he forgot to make the business make sense. He encouraged a variety of shortsighted sales tactics that artificially inflated profits without actually leading to real long-term profits. All his buying and selling, cutting and slashing, couldn't prevent the inevitable. The market figured him out. The numbers hadn't been reflecting the real health of his company.

Once everyone realized what was going on at Sunbeam, the stock plummeted. All the advances made during Al's regime evaporated. In fact, the stock ended up lower than it had been when the board of directors originally called on Al to save the day. And, after a particularly contentious board meeting, Chainsaw Al Dunlap, the man who fired thousands, was fired. There was widespread rejoicing from sources as varied as unemployed ex-Sunbeam plant workers in Louisiana and Troy Dunlap, Al's only son, who, according to *BusinessWeek*, "laughed like hell."

When everyone hates you, from total strangers in the Bayou to your own kids, you know you've been doing something wrong. In this case, what Al Dunlap did wrong was fall in love with a Sacred Cow.

gas

It's easy to fall in love with numbers. We once fell in love with the number 48. We had a glorious summer together, but then we had to go back to school and we fell out of touch. In China, the petroleum conglomerate Sinopec fell in love with numbers—and their larky summer romance ended badly.

In 1998 Sinopec was already one of the biggest companies in China, but they wanted to be bigger. They established an aggressive goal to expand their gas station network. They had numbers in mind, you see. Massive numbers that looked really, really good in the quarterly PowerPoint presentation. So, Sinopec started to expand.

As of 2006, the wholesale Chinese oil market opened up to foreign investment and development. This changed the face of the oil and gas business throughout the country and encouraged competition. But back in 1998 Sinopec was still part of a Chinese oil monopoly. They were one of only five gas-generating options the country had. They had their customers just where they wanted them. There didn't appear to be any impediments to Sinopec's massive expansion plans. They could hit their number for new stations, and their profits couldn't help but increase exponentially.

And expand they did. By 2004, Sinopec had more oil stations in China than anyone else. They hit their number. But the darnedest thing happened . . . they started losing money. At first, everyone was perplexed. They had focused on a number. They had reached that number. How come the rest wasn't taking care of itself?

Further analysis revealed that Sinopec had simply overexpanded. Sure, they had a ton of gas stations. But each gas station was pumping less gas and earning less money than the stations had been before expansion. The drop in revenue coupled with the rise in overhead caused by building and operating so many new stations was hurting the bottom line.

Sinopec immediately stopped expanding and began cutting back their station numbers. They focused instead on large cities and the main highways connecting them. The company began to get healthy again.

Sinopec learned the hard way that if you're going to focus on the numbers, you'd better make sure they're the right numbers.

And numbers, whether they are financials or sales or employee head-counts or gas stations or small appliance totals at Wal-Mart, aren't the goal anyway. Sinopec doesn't sell numbers; they sell gas. You can't make banana bread in numbers—but you can in a Sunbeam bread maker; just ask our grandmothers. Although to do that you'll need a time machine since Nana passed away in 1997. Don't worry though, if we know Sunbeam, they're probably working on one right now.

Teams Create
The Best Solutions

In almost any walk of life, you can't go wrong if you blather on about teamwork. Everybody loves "the team." Even old, fat guys with debilitating asthma who haven't been on skates since they were four get all teary-eyed when you mention the 1980 U.S. Olympic Hockey Team. And this hook, line, and sinker swallowing of the sanctity of the team can be seen in business as well. Jack Welch came down from the mountaintop to tell us to divide ourselves into teams. Productivity would soar, revenues would skyrocket, stock options would quadruple, and all would be right in the world.

Sounds pretty good, huh?

But let's back up a second. Who ran GE for twenty years and who wrote Jack Welch's books? Team Welch? The Welch Wolverines? No. It was Jack Welch, the individual. Granted he had some help with the books, but that was basically typing and spell-checking and stuff. For the most part, Jack Welch's success has been the result of one man—Jack Welch.

Quick—who invented the windshield wiper? Mary Anderson. Who came up with cellophane? Dr. Jacques Edwin Brandenberger. From whence sprang the glory that is the Band-Aid? From the mind of Mr. Earle Dickson, that's from whence.

If you study the history books—or if you just take our word for it—you will discover that most achievements, discoveries, and inventions of lasting importance are the result of individuals. And if you've ever cut yourself while trying to wrap your windshield wipers in cellophane, you'll know what we're talking about.

We're not saying that teams aren't important—we are, after all, a team (although our win-loss record sucks and we're still wearing those dorky '50s short shorts). And we're not downplaying the importance of teamwork. Frankly, we make a pretty significant distinction between "teams" and "teamwork." "Teamwork," people making an effort to work well together, is essential in the development and execution of any good idea/product/Band-Aid. But "teams" rarely come up with these ideas/products/Band-Aids.

Teams tend to foster a herd mentality, which clings to the known instead of embracing the unknown. Teams also tend to head in one of two creative directions: Either they plod along at the pace of their slowest member or they allow themselves to be hijacked by the member with the strongest alpha personality. In those rare moments when the alpha personality belongs to someone like Earle Dickson, the team might come up with the Band-Aid. But usually the alpha guy is just some loudmouth jerk who would be hard-pressed to figure out how to apply a Band-Aid, let alone invent one.

kitchen safety

Back in 1921, Earle Dickson had a problem. His wife, Josephine, kept cutting her fingers while preparing his meals. Exactly why this problem was occurring all the time has been lost in the fog of time. Perhaps Earle ate sushi every day, and his wife was falling victim to the sharp knives and constant slicing. In any case, Earle was tired of tasting blood in his *tekka maki* (or whatever) so he came up with an idea. What if, instead of using the conventional method of applying some gauze to a wound and then wrapping that up with tape, he combined the whole process into one step? That way the protective strip would hold better and be less likely to end up in his *hamachi* (or whatever).

Earle, who worked as a cotton buyer for Johnson & Johnson, put his idea into effect and created the first Band-Aid in short order. His boss saw the invention, realized its effectiveness, and quickly put it into production. Now, if any of us had invented the Band-Aid in our kitchens, we'd probably get hosed on the distribution side. But Earle got lucky and they instantly made him a vice-president of the company.

So, there's a classic example of how the individual can outflank a thousand teams. Imagine all the bull-pen sessions they must have had going at Johnson & Johnson back then where teams of employees were spitballing ideas. In one room everyone waits for the slow guy with the big muttonchops to finish his liverwurst sandwich before explaining to him why they can't go to their bosses with "creamier hand cream." In another room, the hotshot with the loud voice is convincing his coworkers that he has the best idea ever and they have to go to their bosses right now with his all-new, miracle product: "creamier hand cream."

Everyone's watching their back. Everyone's wondering what their bosses will think. Everyone's scared to embarrass themselves. No one wants to risk too much or upset the apple cart. But a few blocks away at the Dickson residence, real innovation is taking place because one guy loves his wife and is tired of eating *unagi* (or whatever) with bloody cotton balls.

That said, teams do serve a vital function in business. And the success of the Band-Aid proves it. Earle came up with a brilliant idea all by himself. But when Johnson & Johnson began marketing it, sales were sluggish. Apparently most Americans weren't plagued by the same issues that were going down in the Dickson home. But the fortunes of the Band-Aid turned around for good when Johnson & Johnson handed out boxes of Band-Aids for free to Boy Scout troops across the country. When the kids started wrapping up their fire-starting blisters and wood-whittling gashes with Band-Aids, the product took off.

Now, history isn't clear on whose idea it was to give away free boxes of Band-Aids to Boy Scouts. But if that doesn't sound like the kind of suggestion a team of brainstorming employees would come up with after a dozen doughnuts and some watered-down coffee, then we don't know anything about teams of brainstorming employees jacked up on cholesterol and caffeine. And that's a possibility. But we're willing to bet that somewhere at Johnson & Johnson, a team came up with an excellent complementary idea to help support and promote the truly brilliant innovation of an individual.

Teams are great at generating consensus. They're wonderful for making people feel like they're a part of what's going on. And they're essential when it comes to execution. They're just not ideally suited for decision making. Unless you think your marketing department can sell "creamier hand cream."

safety safety

And while we're on the subject of obscure geniuses who developed indispensable products due to individual perspicacity and the shunning of "group think," let's chat about Stephanie Louise Kwolek. And before you say "Who?" and go running for the front door of whatever megalithic chain bookstore you're in right now as you debate whether or not to buy this book—and you might as well since you're already on page 57—listen to Stephanie's story and see if it doesn't make you vow to become a rugged individualist and never be part of a team again.

Stephanie was always interested in science. After college she wanted to go on to medical school, but her family couldn't afford it. So she landed a job as a researcher for Du Pont in their textile fibers laboratory and then ended up getting a transfer to Du Pont's Pioneering Research Laboratory in Wilmington, Delaware.

Are you riveted yet? Great. Neither are we. Let's wrap this up.

Stephanie went on to develop all kinds of fascinating and insanely complicated chemical-type stuff. The specifics of pure monomers and synthesized polybenzamides are too mind-shatteringly boring to go into right now. But, basically, Stephanie was part of a team working on new chemical compositions that might lead to marketable products.

Despite being part of a team, however, Stephanie's great contribution was the result of individual skill, luck, and perseverance. While pursuing a line of research that no matter how many times we read about we still can't understand, Stephanie discovered something completely new. It is described as an "aramid polymer." Aside from being weird-sounding, it is generally acknowledged that this aramid polymer was just the kind of discovery that all of her teammates and fellow researchers would have rejected instantly since it was fluid and cloudy instead of viscous and clear. What the scientific world has against the fluid and the cloudy, we cannot even begin to guess. But no one wanted to have anything to do with Stephanie's crazy chemical concoction.

Most researchers would have tossed the murky mess into the trash and moved on to something new. However, instead of just bowing to the will of the team, Stephanie followed her own very individual instincts. She continued on her own to work on the chemical solution and the results were staggering. She succeeded in creating synthetic fibers stronger than anything anyone had ever created before.

Right about now is where the team shows up again. Du Pont got everyone working on how this new miracle invention could be turned into something that the marketing folks could sell. And before you could say "Let's use technology to fundamentally violate the laws of nature," Du Pont was pumping out Kevlar—a fiber five times stronger than steel with half the density of fiberglass.

Du Pont has made hundreds of millions of dollars putting Kevlar in brake pads, radial tires, fiber-optic cable, racing sails, safety helmets, and dozens of other products. But there's one application of Kevlar that trumps all the rest. The next time you see a cop or a soldier who's wearing a bulletproof vest, go up and ask them what they think of Stephanie Louise Kwolek. They'll probably say "Who?" and then shoot you. But thanks to Stephanie Louise Kwolek, you'll be wearing a Kevlar vest also, so you'll be just fine.

Always Focus On
Solving The Problem

Sacred Cows can be sneaky beasts. Sometimes they sound so right and seem to make so much sense that to suggest they be killed makes you sound like a moron. Well, we're not afraid of sounding like morons. The only things we're afraid of are lightning, clowns, and candy that explodes in your mouth. We don't care how incredibly sensible "Always Focus On Solving The Problem" sounds—it's a Sacred Cow and it needs to die.

First of all, that "Always" right there at the beginning is serious trouble. Anytime anyone tells you that something is *always* one way or another, that person is wrong—not always wrong, of course, but usually wrong about always being right. Because we can't just go ahead and say that people are always wrong when they say always because then we'd be saying always too and we'd be just as wrong as the always people. You know what we're talking about, right? Good. Then let's move on.

Focusing on the problem is good. It's the obvious way to fix the problem. If you're leaking coolant from a broken radiator hose, then focusing on the luggage rack isn't going to fix the fact that your car is smoking and you're backing up traffic. Usually, focusing on the problem is the simplest, most straightforward, and effective way of solving what's wrong.

But sometimes what we perceive to be the problem isn't really the root issue that we should be dealing with. And by focusing solely on what we think the problem is, we miss out on a chance to reconfigure the entire paradigm. (Obviously we feel terrible about using the word "paradigm" on this, or any other, occasion.) Let us explain by way of example:

bars

There can be no debate about who is the coolest person ever. The answer is Miles Davis. Please don't bother suggesting alternatives. Miles looked the coolest, he sounded the coolest, he married the coolest women, he wore the coolest clothes, he made the coolest music. The man recorded *Birth of the Cool*, okay? That's how cool he was. He actually gave birth to being cool.

But back around 1946, Miles Davis wasn't quite that cool yet. As a matter of fact, he wasn't even that great a trumpet player. He was good. He was damn good. Good enough to be a member of Charlie Parker's quintet that recorded some of the most important bebop classics ever. But he wasn't quite as good as the masters from whom he learned. And he had a tendency to throttle back his sound, to make small mistakes, and to stumble slightly during his solos.

At that level of virtuosity the difference between good and great is tiny. But Miles knew better. He knew that he just wasn't as good at playing the preferred style of jazz that was packing the clubs and moving sales units. He had a problem on which he had to focus: How do I get better at playing this kind of music?

If Miles danced to the tunes of the Sacred Cows, he would have gone back to Juilliard and blown into his trumpet until his cheeks exploded in a desperate effort to become the best bebop technician ever. But even back then Miles was way too cool to follow the herd. Instead of focusing on the problem, Miles grabbed hold of an opportunity: How can I make the best music possible?

He formed his own band and started playing his own kind of music. He turned away from the complex rhythms and harmonies of bebop and experimented with long melodic lines and modal music. You may have a sneaking suspicion that we have no idea what long melodic lines and modal music are. You are correct. We got most of the specifics from the Internet. But all you have to do is listen to Miles's music and you can hear that it's different.

From 1950 until his death in 1991, Miles Davis made some of the most unique, bizarre, fascinating, and moving records ever. And, ironically, it was his realization of his limitations as a trumpet player that allowed him to make those records. He chose not to waste his time trying to solve what others perceived as a problem. Instead, he let loose his talent and creativity and spawned a whole new sound.

There's a lesson to be learned from Miles Davis: If you kill a Sacred Cow, you will become the coolest person ever.

cars

Jazz trumpet player/stylish cultural touchstone would be one of two careers we'd choose if given the chance to start all over again. The other would be highly paid alternative fuel-source research and development executive at a major car manufacturer. And we're not just saying this because we're about to talk about Larry Burns, a highly paid alternative fuel-source research and development executive at General Motors. We've been big fans of this career path for years. Ask anyone.

But Larry Burns doesn't need our approbation. First of all, he doesn't even know we exist. And, second, he's so busy battling what is arguably the most entrenched corporate environment in the solar system that he doesn't have time to bask in the adulation of a troika of ham-fisted admen/book-wrights.

The people who pay Mr. Burns's salary make their money from gas-powered automobiles. The guys he plays golf with pay their dues with gas money. The thousands of employees who work at his company take home paychecks that, if sniffed very, very closely, might reveal the faint aroma of petroleum. And yet, Larry's whole raison d'être is to figure out how to do away with the traditional gas-burning combustion engine.

Now we don't just bandy about obnoxious French phrases willy-nilly, but this is serious stuff. Global warming, foreign oil dependency—these are some of the most important issues of the day. Usually people who want to do away with the gasoline can be found out in the streets picketing against the newest Hummer or shouting threats from behind a tree somewhere near a G-8 summit. But Larry expresses his radicalism in the boardroom. And, before you get the wrong idea, he's not radical politically, just creatively. He is, after all, a vice president of GM.

So, every day Larry Burns is faced with a problem: "How do we move the car industry away from gas-powered vehicles?" But he has chosen not to focus on that problem. That problem, frankly, just leads to a lot more problems in Larry's world. Instead, Larry has focused on a possibility: "If we were inventing the automobile today, what would we come up with?"

How simple a thought is that and yet how brilliant? In one bold and sassy move, Larry turned a deep-seated worry that causes nothing but headaches for everyone in his field into a call for innovation, creativity, and significant potential financial remuneration.

Larry knows that his fellow car company people would rather not think about any kind of change, especially wild sea changes like shifting to hydrogen fuel cells. As he puts it, "I know fuel cells are a disruptive technology. But we have to attack ourselves." We always thought that attacking ourselves would lead to blindness, but Larry has proved us wrong. He has helped push General Motors to the international forefront of alternative fuel development.

Larry has been running GM's R&D division for almost a decade, and you may have noticed that we're not all driving around in hydrogen fuel cell–powered cars. In fact, no one is. But under Larry's watch, fuel-cell development (as well as other, nontraditional methods of powering vehicles) has steadily moved forward. Where others have failed and slipped back into the morass of conventional thinking, Larry has persevered. Does he deserve to be sainted by the environmentalists for changing the face of the automobile industry? No. Does he deserve to be commended for attempting to solve an almost insurmountable problem by focusing on the possibilities it creates? Yes. Does he ever wear denim jackets with jeans? Never.

Sometimes obvious problems demand obvious solutions. If your radiator hose is cracked, you must replace it with a new radiator hose. But sometimes what we perceive to be the problem is just a symptom of something not working on a much larger scale. We can't let those damn Cows browbeat us into submissiveness. Maybe we should be like Miles Davis and Larry Burns more often. When we're standing by the side of the highway waving at smoke and choking on chemical fumes, we should start thinking like those guys.

Maybe there's something wrong with the whole radiator. Or maybe cars don't really even need radiators. Maybe there's some kind of systemic cooling system made out of dry ice and popsicle sticks that could keep your car from overheating and serve raspberry daiquiris at the same time. Who knows what kind of miraculous, world-changing, and moneymaking ideas we could come up with if we stopped focusing on the problem all the time and started focusing on the possibilities?

Follow The Leader

In business, there are leaders and there are followers. There are winners and there are losers. There are companies that go public for billions, and there are others that go bankrupt in weeks. These are facts.

Our receptionist's daughter is nine years old and goes to one of those progressive, touchy-feely schools where there are no grades, Christmas doesn't exist, and no one ever wins or loses anything. She can whittle wood like a pro and her self-esteem is through the roof, but we're a little worried about her ability to survive in the business world. Fortunately she fully expects to become a professional soccer player/chef/cartoon voice-over actress so she probably won't have to slug it out in the corporate trenches. But what about the rest of us?

What can we do to get ahead? How can we achieve success? What's the quickest way to the top of the ladder? For a lot of people the answer is clear—Follow The Leader.

This thought makes a certain amount of sense. Find out who's number one in your field and then copy his or her path to victory. If it worked for him or her, then it ought to work for you too. But does this thought really hold water? A little, maybe. Possibly enough for a small rhododendron. But not enough for a whole Sacred Cow.

Categories are constantly remade in the likeness of the

category leader. They're in control now, so they can change the rules to suit their needs. By copying them, you're playing a game that they invented and have had more time to excel at.

Ultimately, every one of us needs to come up with our own definition of success. And the way to achieve it is going to be uniquely personal as well. Copying someone else's success will rarely lead to achieving your own. But don't take our word for it. After all, we just downed a brandy snifter filled with cold medicine and we're making about as much sense as Daffy Duck with Tourette's syndrome. Allow us to prove our point with an illustrative example.

ball

Stephon Marbury has a problem—and it's not just that the Knicks stink. Stephon's problem is that the Knicks stink and pretty much everyone blames him for it. Whether that's fair or not, it feeds into an even larger problem—Stephon Marbury is universally acknowledged by the basketball cognoscenti to be a total head case. He has perfected the fine art of sulking and has achieved Ph.D. level success in surliness, lack of communication, and undermining his coaches in the press. He is strong, fast, and can score at will, but he has never led a team past the first round of the playoffs. Even worse, every team from which he has been traded has improved dramatically after he left.

So, what does a guy like this do if he wants to rehabilitate his image? He sells some sneakers.

"Hold it!" you shout while spitting out an unchewed chunk of veal marsala. "All those NBA stars sell sneakers. Stephon Marbury is just Following The Leader!"

Relax. Cut your food into smaller pieces. Let us explain.

In the past, Stephon has been guilty of Following The Leader. He came into the League, saw the success of guys like Michael Jordan and went right out and signed a big ol' sneaker deal with And 1. He released his signature shoes, charged the traditional $100 plus for them, and waited for the additional riches to roll in.

But the shoes never sold that well. Some might blame And 1, their faulty marketing campaign and rickety corporate structure. But most people would blame Stephon and his lack of success on and off the court for his sneakers' so-so sales.

By the time Stephon came to the Knicks he had left And 1 and was dealing with bad press, a lousy reputation, and losing seasons.

So he released another line of signature sneakers. However, instead of just Following the Leader, this time he did something completely original. Whereas LeBron James's new kicks retail for around $150, Stephon's sneakers sell for $14.98. That's less than a pepperoni pizza (and you can't run the fast break with pizza on your feet). In fact, Marbury released a whole line of sportswear, and the *most expensive* item available was the sneakers.

He did it to help lower-income kids feel like they can afford something cool and special. He can make money on the deal only if the shoes become astronomically successful. But, more important, Stephon redefined his own vision of success. He wanted to do something positive for kids. He did it. He probably also wanted to get some good press for a change. He did that too.

The Knicks still stink, but Stephon Marbury succeeded on his own terms by Not Following The Leader. That said— we would trade Steph for LeBron straight up any day of the week.

flight

Following The Leader isn't just a kid's game that we have never seen anyone play in real life and probably exists only in the film and theater versions of *Peter Pan*. It's also a business practice that has infiltrated every corner of the world of commerce and industry.

In the mid-'90s, Southwest Airlines entered the East Coast market. Almost immediately the other airlines began to sweat. Southwest had already established a reputation for dominance in the other regions in which they flew. The established East Coast service providers were desperate to prevent that from happening in their own backyards.

So, what did they do? They Followed The Leader. They attempted to copy Southwest's strategies in an effort to keep them out of their markets. First Continental offered "lite" service on certain routes that Southwest was competing for. But Continental's overhead was much higher than Southwest's. Within a year they had lost a ton of money and given up. They dropped the "lite" service and abandoned the dream of ever beating Southwest.

US Airways also tried to compete with Southwest by copying them. They introduced a Southwest-y service called Metrojet. But they couldn't match costs either, and within two years they folded their metaphorical tent as well.

Continental and US Airways committed the cardinal sin of Following the Leader when they should have been trying to differentiate themselves from the leader. Other airlines figured this out and used it to great success.

Alaska Airlines never tried to Follow The Leaders. They weren't interested in becoming the best airline in the skies. They just wanted to be the best airline for Alaska. By focusing on that simple but worthwhile goal, they quickly became just that. Alaska Airlines dominates all air travel to and from Alaska.

JetBlue is another airline that purposely didn't Follow The Leader. They found a way to create a unique and completely different flying experience. They would identify high-travel routes and then sell tickets on brand-new planes with leather seats and DirecTV all for a discount price. Flying JetBlue quickly became a different experience from flying with other airlines. And they were phenomenally successful.

Sometimes Following The Leader can be an effective strategy. If you're just starting out in business, copying the successful strategies of the category leader can help you close the gap. And sometimes you can Follow The Leader so successfully that you become the Leader and everyone suddenly starts Following You. But, in general, finding a way to promote what makes you different and special is the best way to achieve your goals of wealth, fame, and world domination.

Success Breeds
Success

Contrary to the opinion of our high school football coach, we are not made of stone. We think, we feel, we laugh, we cry. And we care, damn it! We care about some of these Sacred Cows even though it is our solemn duty to kill them until they are dead. Sometimes there's a tear in our eye as we pull the trigger. And "Success Breeds Success" is one of those Cows that it hurts to eliminate. Because we used to believe in this one—big-time.

"Success Breeds Success" was basically our dating mantra throughout the '80s. One well-crafted pickup line inevitably and inexorably led to another and another until we had a fistful of phone numbers. Sometimes, when success was really breeding success, the evening would end up with more than phone numbers. Sometimes the evening would end up with breakfast, if you know what we mean (and we hope you do because we're not spelling it out any clearer—our mothers may be reading this).

So, yes—success appeared to breed success in the seedy watering holes of our youth. But does success breed success in the business world? Does it always lead to success? And most significantly, is it a mistake to work from the assumption that just because someone or something has been successful once, he or she or it is more likely to be successful again? According to our research—which has a scientifically established margin of error of only one/one thousandth of the square root of pi (or roughly the thickness of thinly sliced *prosciutto*)—the answers to these queries are: sometimes, no, and yes.

tempus fugit

In the Olde Days of Yore, there were certain irrefutable facts: the world was flat, bloodletting was a sound medical practice, and the Swiss made the best watches. Well, nowadays we know better. The world is roundish, bloodletting is effective only if one uses the very best leeches, and the Swiss completely blew their worldwide watchmaking monopoly.

The cornerstone upon which the Swiss built their temple of timekeeping was the mechanical movement. All those crazy gears and cogs and coils and springs—that's Switzerland, baby. For centuries the Swiss made the most watches and the best watches—all with mechanical movements. The watch business was extremely successful. And success bred success.

The Swiss have always been on the cutting edge of product development and new technologies. While still churning out hundreds of thousands of mechanical movement-based watches, they also discovered alternative methods for driving their machinery. In the 1960s, Swiss researchers invented the quartz movement and the tuning fork movement—both of which kept watches ticking even more accurately than the mechanical movements.

So, here we are in the latter third of the twentieth century and the Swiss are dominating the watch market in every facet on a global scale. That's success, right? And it's supposed to breed more success, right? Well, tell that to the Japanese.

The Seiko Company of Japan had been making mechanical movement watches for a while, but they were small potatoes compared to the Swiss firms. But they took a look at what was happening in Europe and made a bold decision: they were going to drop the mechanical movement part of their business to focus on making low-cost, high-quality watches using quartz movements.

Almost immediately, Seiko was hugely successful. Sales were so strong that they changed the face of the watch industry worldwide. Suddenly, everyone was making smaller, lighter, less-expensive watches featuring quartz movements. And they were selling like hot cakes. Frankly, they were selling better than hot cakes because the profit margins were greater and they had more advertising dollars than the hot cake industry.

The Swiss, however, refused to jump on the quartz bandwagon. Even though they invented these new movement technologies, the Swiss steadfastly remained committed to making watches with mechanical movements. Mechanical movements are fundamentally cool with their intricate details and complex workings, but they're expensive to produce and they're notoriously less reliable than quartz movements. Not surprisingly, with each passing year, Switzerland's share of the global watch market shrunk.

Perhaps the Swiss considered quartz movements to be aesthetically inferior. Or perhaps their years of success breeding success conditioned them to believe that continued success was inevitable. Whatever the reason, the Japanese shattered the Swiss watch hegemony. Fortunately for the Swiss, however, they still have excellent banks and chocolate.

monster truck

A few paces to the right and a quick scoot downhill from Switzerland, one arrives in India. On the subcontinent, you can find the answers to a great many puzzlements. Want to know the difference between an Indian elephant and an African elephant? Go to India (or Africa). Want to know why cricket isn't the most boring game on Earth? Go to India (although it is the most boring game on Earth). Want to know why blindly buying into the Sacred Cow "Success Breeds Success" is a foolish business policy? Go to India (or buy this book).

Hyundai is a Korean car manufacturer with a firm grip on almost every sector of the Indian automobile market. Almost 20% of the cars purchased in India are Hyundais. They launched the midsized Hyundai Accent, and it was a huge success. They introduced the smaller-sized Santro, and it was an even huger success.

It was only natural that Hyundai's next move would be to tap into the top-end SUV market. The Hyundai folk figured that it had a slam dunk on its hands. SUVs are extremely popular these days. Hyundai had proven time and time again that they knew exactly what kinds of cars to make for and promote to the Indian consumers. And they were major players in the Indian automobile market. Obviously their previous successes would lead to even greater success for Terracan, their new SUV.

Hyundai launched a massive ad campaign. They bought airtime, billboards, magazine and newspaper ads. They made sure that all of India knew that the Terracan was coming. Luxurious interior, confident handling, impressive ground clearance, reliable motor—the Hyundai PR machine danced and gamboled and dazzled and pleaded just as they did whenever they were pushing a new product.

But the damnedest thing happened . . . nobody in India bought it. Not only did they not buy the hype that Hyundai was selling, they didn't buy the car Hyundai was selling. And not only did they "not buy it," they *really* didn't buy it.

In 2005, Hyundai sold a grand total of two hundred Terracans in India. *Two hundred!* There are over one billion people in India. With that huge a consumer base, you should be able to sell more than two hundred of anything just by accident. They should have moved more units on impulse buys alone. How often have you been at the checkout line at the supermarket and you bought one of those idiotic celebrity magazines just 'cause it was there and you were bored? With more than a billion people wandering around, our complex purchasing graphs indicate that at least five hundred of them should have been bored, found themselves in front of a Hyundai dealership, and bought a Terracan just for the hell of it.

But that's not what happened. Terracan totally bombed. And it's not a question of wrong fit in the marketplace. Terracan may have been overpriced and burned a lot of gas, but a lot of other car manufacturers were having success with high-end SUVs at the same time that Terracan was floundering.

Why was the Terracan such a dismal failure? There's no clear answer to that question. Perhaps Hyundai just got unlucky. Perhaps a variety of bizarre circumstances coalesced at an inopportune moment. But it does seem like Hyundai got caught in the trap of "Success Breeding Success." They just assumed that Terracan would work in India because all their previous models had worked in India. But you have to earn your success each time out. You can never take the future for granted. And you need to learn from your mistakes.

Hyundai failed the first two tests before they launched Terracan. And it looks like they failed the third test after the Terracan debacle. In a recent list of unsuccessful brand launches in India, Hyundai reared its head again. Only, instead of Terracan, the list mentioned their newer, smaller SUV—Tucson.

Yup. That's right. After the disaster of Terracan, Hyundai went off, licked its wounds, and came back with another new brand, the Tucson. And it was a monumental failure also. Now, we're not trying to create a new Sacred Cow called "Failure Breeds Failure." We just wanted to point out that no one can predict the future and you can never take success for granted. Also, you should never wear a fanny pack.

fallen arches

And speaking of double denim, otherwise known as the Canadian Tuxedo, let's talk about McDonald's. What's the connection? Well, the Scottish were instrumental in the development of Canada—Nova Scotia means "New Scotland" after all (or at least that's what the nuns taught us). And McDonald's sounds Scottish. Or maybe it's Irish. Whatever it is, we're going to talk about McDonald's with or without a smooth transition. Because when it comes to debunking that shadowy canard Success Breeds Success, you need look no further than the Golden Arches.

We have neither the time nor the inclination to chart the progress of the global phenomenon into which Ray Kroc's simple idea evolved. Suffice it to say that in the Venn diagram of life, McDonald's is the little shaded area where everything and everyone intersects. Not us, frankly. We can't stand the smell of the place. But the rest of the known universe seems to eat there pretty regularly.

They made burgers, and the burgers sold. They made fries; they flew out the window. Chicken sandwiches, milk shakes, McNuggets, you name it. McDonald's made it, and the people bought it. The company appeared to prove and reprove on a daily basis that Success Breeds Success.

And then one bright sunny day, or perhaps it was raining—

our 1996 almanac is missing some pages—someone over at corporate headquarters had a brilliant idea. If you were a fly on the wall at that meeting, you might have heard the following: "Hey, get that fly off the wall! This is a restaurant—kind of!" You almost might have heard, "It's time for McDonald's to appeal to an older, more sophisticated, upscale clientele. It's time to introduce the Arch Deluxe."

The Arch Deluxe is what happens when smart, successful people get together and convince themselves that since they've always been smart and successful in the past, they'll always be smart and successful in the future. The Arch Deluxe and the Bay of Pigs Invasion. Everyone at McDonald's was so sure that targeting an older, wealthier demographic was such a "can't miss" idea that they geared up their potent marketing machine and aimed it at the American public.

For a while back in 1996, the Arch Deluxe was everywhere you looked. TV spots, magazine ads, bus billboards—it was as omnipresent as Howie Mandel. But when the product line was finally released, the darnedest thing happened: the Arch Deluxe was a total bomb. At first it was widely sampled, the ad campaign made sure of that. But once folks tasted the thing, they didn't want any more.

Perhaps it was because the price point was too high. Perhaps the consumers were becoming a little more health conscious and they shied away from the higher fat content in the Arch Deluxe sandwiches. Or perhaps Andrew Selvaggio, the executive chef hired by McDonald's to craft these tasty treats, simply produced a variety of unpleasant tastes between two sesame seed buns. For whatever the reasons, the Arch Deluxe was a colossal disaster. The media campaign cost over $100 million and McDonald's had to discontinue the entire product line.

Just because you hit a home run once doesn't mean you're

going to hit a home run every time. Just because you captivate the free world with your toothy grin and Boston accent doesn't mean that a ragtag bunch of exiled Cuban nationals should attempt to invade a Caribbean island. And just because you've sold everything and anything to a hungry nation on a budget doesn't mean you can overcharge them for foul-tasting, pseudo-sophisticated meat patties. Success doesn't always breed success. Sometimes it breeds indigestion.

The Gate Strikes Back:
Five Sacred Cows Of Advertising

2. Don't Ask The Reader To Think

At times advertising suffers from the same low opinion of the public's intelligence as do the entertainment industry, the medical field, law, politics, and just about everything else. Sometimes they have a point. A moronic jingle with an infectious tune that rhymes "fizz fizz" with "what a relief it is" can stay in your brain forever while Brahms's subtle and nuanced Concerto in D Major is almost impossible to hum in the shower. Sometimes, however, challenging your target audience is the quickest way to winning their hearts. The Geico ads featuring the aggrieved Cavemen are an example of dense and somewhat off-topic spots that make the viewer think. Who are these people? What's really going on here? What the hell does any of this have to do with car insurance? Whether or not viewers satisfactorily answer any of these questions, they think, they laugh, and they know it all has something to do with something called Geico—and that's good advertising.

Marketing Should
Follow Company Strategy,
Not Drive It

We'll be honest with you (for a refreshing change of pace): When we hear the word "marketing," we immediately think of curvaceous suburban moms squeezing cantaloupes in the produce section of an airplane-hangar-sized Super Stop & Shop. This may have more to do with unfulfilled adolescent fantasies than it does with the absurdity of the business world—but not by much. Because business marketing has become such a muddled, overwrought, and overthought concept that it makes us yearn for the simplicity of squeaky cart wheels on linoleum floors and seeing how much bulk candy we can shovel into our mouths before getting yelled at by the guy behind the meat counter with the blood-spattered smock. And you know whose blood that is, right? That's cow blood. Bloody Smock Guy may have been weird and wildly unhygienic, but he was on the front lines of Sacred Cow killing and for that we salute him.

When it comes to marketing, there are a lot of Sacred Cows in dire need of being slaughtered. For the sake of time, however, we will do away with only three of them. But if you bump into us at the mall, feel free to ask us to kill some others for you while we desperately try to remember where we parked our Microbus. The first evil Marketing Cow is Marketing Should Follow Company Strategy, Not Drive It. Brace yourselves for its imminent death.

bufonis (toads)

Marketing gets short shrift in the business world, and we firmly believe that much, much longer shrifts are called for. As we mentioned two brief paragraphs ago, we're being honest now and we want you to be honest with us. Reach down deep into the most truthful part of your soul just past the part that still believes in the Easter Bunny and answer the following question: Is the product you're selling truly different from the competition? Don't feed us the corporate mumbo jumbo, just answer the question with total candor.

If you're like 98% of the people out there, your answer should be, "Er . . . no. Not really." And that's okay. It's not necessary to be a trendsetter or trailblazer to succeed in the business world. It's also not necessary to do any kind of scientific research in order to assert that 98% of businesspeople acknowledge that their products are very, very similar to the competition's. We completely invented that number just now. But it sure feels like most items, brands, and services have a whole lot in common and not so many profound differences.

So what makes one product stand out while its many, almost identical brethren end up gathering dust in the basement of the 99 Cent Store? Why are Nike and Adidas on top of the world while Avia and Spot-Bilt are just quizzical memories from the '80s? (Yes, we're aware that both Avia and Spot-Bilt are still in business, but they're not exactly capturing the public's imagination, are they? They had their moment in the sun, and now they're just plodding along the murky fringes of Sneaker Universe.)

The whats and whys can be succinctly answered with one word: marketing. Of all the key components to business success, marketing is probably the most underappreciated. The sales department gets the glory, but without marketing they can't even do their jobs effectively. How are they going to sell something that nobody has heard of or cares about? Marketing lets everyone know who you are, what you have to offer, and creates the illusion that they can't live without you. Yet too many businesses put sales on a pedestal and marketing in a stained milk carton just below the pedestal and to the right a little.

Remember a few years ago when all those Internet start-ups suddenly sprouted like mushrooms in a dank, dark cave? A few of them grew into insanely successful companies. The rest of them shriveled and died like old men in a really hot sauna. For the most part, the ones that worked had C-level marketing executives driving the show. The failures put all their eggs in the sales basket and forget to build a strong marketing department.

Marketing makes the difference between otherwise similar products. Case in point—booze. We're no strangers to the grape and the grain. And our palates are notoriously acute. In fact, we once won forty dollars by picking out Hellmann's mayonnaise in a blind taste test. But we simply cannot distinguish between most mass-produced American beers in a can. We have tried. Believe us, we have tried. We have tried pretty much every Friday night after work for the past fifteen years. But no matter how much we drink and drink and drink, all those big-time American brews taste exactly the same to us.

Most beer drinkers agree. Even people who swear allegiance to one brand or another often can't differentiate between their "favorite" and another company's swill in blind taste tests (much like the Great Mayonnaise Challenge of 2003). In terms of flavor, price, and quality, there is true parity in the world of mass-produced, mass-marketed American beer.

So what possible reason could there be for the significant

sales spike that Budweiser enjoyed in the mid- to late-'90s? If their beer tastes pretty much like Michelob and Coors and Miller, and they all cost about the same, how come so many people suddenly decided to buy a lot of Bud? The answer: Frogs.

During Super Bowl XXIX in 1995 (remember when Steve Young went bananas and threw for six touchdowns?) Budweiser launched its first commercial featuring the Budweiser Frogs. Those idiotic Frogs who croaked out the three syllables "Bud," "Weis," and "Er" became an overnight sensation. They were featured in dozens of commercials, they spawned a massive Internet hoax, and they were even condemned by an organization devoted to temperance. That's really the trifecta of American cultural iconography: stardom, viral Internet success, and inciting the rage of picketing conservatives.

These three Frogs and the many other heart-stoppingly adorable creatures who performed in subsequent commercials were directly responsible for significant increases in Budweiser sales. Budweiser did not suddenly improve the taste of their beer in 1995. They didn't lower their prices or prove scientifically that drinking Budweiser would make you live longer or perform better in the sack. They simply employed an ingenious marketing campaign that coaxed millions of Americans into drinking their suds.

The marketing drove the business; it did not react to changes in the business. The advertisers who created the spots were not programmed to respond to company-wide mission statements and sales goals. They were just a bunch of creative people with a weird idea: Let's use animated Frogs to sell Budweiser beer. Someone took a chance on a clever marketing strategy, and the rest is incredibly annoying history.

The Goal Of
Marketing Is To
Sell A Product

Here's our second Sacred Cow Of Marketing—The Goal Of Marketing Is To Sell A Product. That sure sounds sensible, no? Are we seriously suggesting that this statement is incorrect? Do we have the gall to imply that the goal of marketing *isn't* to sell a product? And if we have that gall, where do we keep it? In a small wooden structure in the yard or do we let our gall sleep in the house? All valid questions, and you're perfectly right to raise them. Because the goal of marketing is to sell a product . . . sometimes. Sometimes you need to unload your kid's violin because he doesn't want to play anymore, so you put up a sign at the post office saying, "Used Violin for Sale!" The violin is the product. The sign is the marketing. Pretty straightforward, right? But business tends to be a little more complex than that (except for businesses that only sell used kids' violins). And, more often than not, the goal of marketing shouldn't be to sell a product—but to *attract customers*.

Why did we italicize *attract customers*? (Look, we did it again!) We didn't just do it because our computers can make it happen with an effortless click of a button—although we probably wouldn't have done it if it entailed hard work. We italicized those two words because *they're the important ones*.

In the age-old debate between "Attract" and "Sell," we come down firmly on the side of attraction, which is why we either shave every day or keep our beards neat and tidy. You can sell one item to one person and that's a viable business model. But doesn't it make more sense to attract a lot of people to a whole range of products? Wouldn't that be a more lucrative long-term business model? Why, yes, it would. Thanks for asking.

calcei (shoes)

One delightfully illustrative paradigm for the attract versus sell issue as it pertains to marketing is the rivalry between Nike and adidas (why don't they capitalize adidas?). Nike and adidas have been the two biggest athletic shoe manufacturers ever since the tenth century when the Visigoths invaded Wyoming. But things really started heating up in the mid-1980s.

In 1984, Nike began a partnership with an athlete who would change the world of sports, sporting goods, and male-pattern baldness forever—Michael Jordan. As his popularity quickly grew, Nike made sure that everyone knew about him and his new sneakers. During the All-Star Game, he wore his brand-new Nikes even though the NBA fined him because they were considered "too colorful." And the nonstop Air Jordan marketing push began. Soon it seemed like every TV set, magazine page, and bus stop was demanding that we shell out our hard-earned cash to be like Mike.

Around the same time, adidas landed a very different kind of marketing coup. While MJ bounced around in his Air Jordans on his way to becoming the greatest basketball player/shoe salesman of all time, adidas found themselves selling lots of sneakers thanks to three guys from Queens with no shoelaces but an excellent rhyming thesaurus.

Run-D.M.C.'s *Raising Hell* sold over three million copies and every single one of them featured a song called "My Adidas" on track number three. The tune was a profoundly imbecilic ode to a particular brand of tennis shoes that Run and D.M.C. (not to mention Jam Master Jay) liked to wear. As the fellas so aptly put it, "My adidas and me, close as can be, we make a mean team, my adidas and me."

Adidas didn't pay these guys to rap about their sneakers. They probably had no idea that Joseph Simmons and Darryl McDaniels were traipsing around the world's concert halls wearing their product. And they never could have predicted that a whole hip-hop fashion world would spring up and embrace laceless black and white adidas as the apotheosis of "must have" footwear. All adidas knew was that they were selling lots of shoes. Run-D.M.C. did more to help adidas weather the Jordan-fueled Nike storm than any hard-sell ad campaign could ever have done.

Michael Jordan was hired by Nike to sell a product. And that strategy certainly worked, although it cost them a medium-sized fortune. Run-D.M.C. and the advent of b-boy fashion attracted huge numbers of consumers to the adidas brand. And it didn't cost the company a dime. Sure, adidas spent a lot of money on other kinds of traditional marketing aimed at pushing their products at customers. But this one incidental confluence of product placement and cultural zeitgeist created an attractive buying atmosphere that gave adidas a level of street credibility that no amount of hard-driving ads could have purchased. That may have been the most dense and convoluted sentence we have ever written. But we stand by it. We stand by it in unlaced adidas that we have been cleaning religiously with an electric toothbrush every Sunday afternoon since 1986.

And that's how to keep it real.

Marketing Should
Always Be Direct

This is our third and final Marketing Cow, and it's about time, eh? The idea that Marketing Should Always Be Direct has been around even longer than Direct Marketing—and, frankly, both of them can take a hike. As a matter of fact, both of them can take a hike through a remote national park in the middle of winter, fall into a snow-filled ravine, get frostbite, panic, and eat each other.

Businesspeople always want to be direct. It must be part of that whole "look 'em in the eye and shake their hands firmly" ethos. Like drinking six martinis for lunch, voting for Eisenhower, and wearing a derby all the time, that kind of thinking belongs to a bygone era (we think it's the Golden Age of France, but we're not sure).

Being direct does not mean being effective. It *can* mean that. Sometimes the direct approach is the best approach. But more often than not, bending an idea slightly, adding some nuance, a touch of style, a soupçon of cleverness, and a light dusting of the unexpected leads to the most successful marketing campaigns.

People often ask us why this is so. "Why can't we just be direct?" they implore us with big, saucer eyes and quivering lips. And we have a good answer for this. We just don't tell them until their eyes return to normal size and their lips reach an acceptable level of stasis.

When it comes to marketing and advertising, being boring, plain, and direct presupposes that the people to whom you are marketing actually care about your product. Obviously *you* care about your product. But what is the likelihood that the family of Swedish immigrants who have gathered around the TV set to enjoy a hearty meal of meatballs and apricot nectar care? That likelihood is small. It's smaller than Danny DeVito.

So, instead of just laying out the basics of what you're marketing, you need to make that marketing moment special. You need to make it memorable. You need to make it linger and grow to the point where those juice-stained Swedes can't remember a time when they weren't captivated by whatever crap you're trying to sell them.

pax et lacto (peace and milk)

This principle doesn't just work in the business world. Throughout time, the successful marketing of ideas has proven that being straightforward and obvious is rarely as successful as being nuanced and thought-provoking. Take John F. Kennedy, for example. During his inauguration speech, one of the ideas that he wanted to convey was that Americans were becoming a spoiled and selfish lot and they needed to start giving back to the community. He didn't say that, however. Instead he crafted the elegantly obtuse sentence, "Ask not what your country can do for you; ask what you can do for your country."

That rich and textured line gave birth to the Peace Corps. By purposefully not being direct, John F. Kennedy's message became memorable, even immortal. The obvious version of that speech might have been forgotten as just another dull bit of political posturing. The indirect version launched one of the great humanitarian organizations of the twentieth century.

Not to trivialize JFK, the Peace Corps, or dairy products, but the same thinking that informed the president led to the creation of the hugely successful "Got Milk?" campaign. Obviously what the Dairy Association really wanted to say—what they'd say if they wanted to be direct—was "Get Milk!" But changing the "e" to an "o" and swapping out the exclamation point for a question mark was a brilliant bit of subterfuge.

The subtlety, originality, and whimsy of that campaign instantly turned it into a pop cultural touchstone. It didn't give birth to the Peace Corps, but it probably conned a lot of kids into drinking milk instead of soda. And we're big fans of anything that hits dentists right in the wallet.

Only Hire Someone
Who Has Done
The Job Before

Some Sacred Cows are easier to kill than others. The ones based on well-reasoned arguments and time-honored business traditions go down hard. This one, however, could be whacked by our IT guy's eight-year-old niece. Of course, she's a champion Muay Thai boxer who has killed at least ten men that we know of—but you get our point. If you only hired someone who had done the job before, then how did the very first people in the very first jobs get hired? Right? So, that's it, right? Everyone is going to stop believing in this one now and we can finish our hot cocoa and take a well-deserved nap, right?

Not right.

This Sacred Cow persists in almost every business, and it will continue to cling tenaciously to the corporate psyche. Obviously, when time began and the first protozoa staggered out of the brackish fen, donned suspenders, and headed for roughly hewn stone caveman offices, it was okay to hire neophytes. But now that we've all been around awhile and you can pretty much count on someone somewhere having already done some version of whatever you need done, no one wants to hire a novice.

Their reasons are invariably sound: "Why take the risk?" "There's no substitute for experience." "Napoleon already invaded Russia once and he knows where all the good restaurants are—we have to get him to do it again!"

Hiring someone who has done it before is easier in a lot of ways. That person knows the ropes and they're less likely to disagree with you. They're attuned to the vicissitudes of the business world and they probably won't shake the tree or rattle the cage or whatever other lame metaphor you want to plug in there. But is making that safe hire making the *best* hire? Is experience more valuable than ingenuity and initiative? Should you really be following the path of least resistance? If you're an aerospace engineer specializing in streamlining spacecraft, you probably should be following the path of least resistance. Everyone else should follow us to the next paragraph as we delve more deeply.

tragedy

Ben Sliney was an air traffic controller and a lawyer who once sued the Federal Aviation Administration on behalf of the air traffic controllers. It was a little surprising, therefore, that he ended up taking a job with the FAA as National Operations Manager. He had never held any position like the one he now had.

His first day on his new job turned out to be September 11, 2001. Within minutes of arriving at the command center (of which he was now in command), reports of the hijackings started hitting his desk. As the events of the day quickly spiraled out of control, Sliney was under tremendous pressure to do something, anything, to try to minimize the potential for escalating disaster.

What he did was unprecedented in the history of American aviation. He ordered every single plane in the air to land immediately, and he completely closed the skies. No one had ever taken this step before. An Operations Manager with years of experience might not have made the same move. They almost certainly wouldn't have done it as quickly.

As Sliney said in *USA Today*, "It was good that I was there and not someone more in tune with the bureaucracy." Sliney was new to the job and the corporate culture of the FAA. But he thought on his feet and went with his instincts. Grounding those planes may have saved thousands of lives. Fortunately, the FAA hired someone who hadn't done the job before.

comedy

Okay, that's it for the sad and serious stuff. Now let's prove our point with a light and goofy example. Preferably a bald, light, and goofy example with glasses, a lousy golf swing, and hundreds of millions of dollars in the bank. Let's prove our point with Larry David.

Show business operates by many bizarre and anachronistic rules that would seem downright idiotic to the normal and the sane. Fortunately, the normal and the sane are vastly outnumbered in Hollywood by agents and development executives. Show business is, however, a business (it's right there in the title), and it does bow before the same Sacred Cows as everyone else.

Much like professional football coaches, the men and women chosen to create and executive-produce sitcoms are drawn from an incredibly small pool. It's like one of those tiny inflatable pools with the protruding palm tree—only this one is filled with funny millionaires. Sitcoms, while fundamentally idiotic, cost a lot of money. In success, they generate a lot, lot more. So, the powers that be are extremely selective about who gets to pilot these artificial laugh-filled ships.

One of the most important criteria for these "show runners" is that they have done the job before. Hollywood is a firm believer in the "Only Hire Someone Who Has Done the Job Before" credo.

So, when Larry David and his pal, Jerry Seinfeld, sold their show, *The Seinfeld Chronicles*, to NBC, they knew that something had to give. Jerry was the talent (although he also helped write). And Larry was the writer (although he also occasionally performed in the show). The problem was that Larry had never run a sitcom before. He hadn't even worked on a sitcom before. He was a mediocre stand-up comedian who had written briefly on *Saturday Night Live*. That was it.

NBC decided to put the show on the air, but they weren't going to let Larry be the boss. They hired him as a producer on the show he had created and loaded up the payroll with a variety of executive producers with "experience."

One of these experienced gentlemen went off and did a rewrite of Larry's pilot without his knowledge. When he found out about it, Larry threatened to quit (this is the first of 600 times that Larry threatened to quit—601 if you count the time that he actually did quit).

NBC convinced Larry not to quit by essentially allowing him to run the show. They didn't make him an executive producer, they didn't give him more money, and they still kept all those people above him on the pyramid of power, but they basically said—take a shot and let's see what happens.

What happened is the guy ended up generating nine hundred bazillion dollars for everyone who even came within a stone's throw of the *Seinfeld* set. The network cashed in, the studio cashed in, he and Jerry cashed in, all those executive producers with experience who didn't really do anything cashed in—the crafts services lady probably got rich.

The phenomenal success of *Seinfeld* was due in large part to its unique voice and tone—both of which sprang from the almost hairless head of Larry David. Some sitcom show-runner hack with ten other series under his belt might have turned *Seinfeld* into just another forgettable yawn fest. But specifically because Larry had never done the job before, he was able to do it in a completely new and original way.

And now he owns half of Los Angeles. Arnold Schwarzenegger —another successful individual who had no experience at either of his two post-bodybuilding professions—owns the other half.

Everyone Deserves
A Second Chance

You know what? We almost left this Sacred Cow alone. Because everyone does deserve a second chance. There's no one out there, not even the most incorrigible reprobate, who hasn't deserved a second chance at least once in his or her life. Take Joseph Stalin, for example. Not a good guy. Some consider him the most despicable figure of the twentieth century—and that's really saying something, as the competition was fierce. But at some point in Stalin's childhood, he probably messed up and deserved a break. He might have tried to deep-fry a *pierogi*, slipped on some *gorchitsa*, and accidentally scalded the family *sobaka*. His dad probably called him an *ozornik*, gave him a *pobol* in the *pishchevol*, and sent him to bed without any *drachona* or *pirozhky*. We, however, would have given him a second chance because, at the time, he was just a kid making an innocent mistake.

Ultimately, however, we decided to kill this Sacred Cow because it is responsible for a tremendous amount of business malaise and corporate foolishness. True: Everyone deserves a second chance. Untrue: Everyone deserves a second chance all the time. Just because there are situations in which it makes sense to give someone another try to succeed doesn't mean you should always give someone another try to succeed. It's important to differentiate between appropriate and inappropriate second chance opportunities.

There should be some kind of second chance credit checking system that keeps up-to-date records on how many breaks you have already received. We should also come up with a color-coded rating system to establish the potential ramifications of giving someone a second chance. Young Stalin probably should have had another opportunity to fry those dumplings. Old Stalin definitely should not have had another opportunity to starve the Ukraine.

We have no idea how we got off the subject of business and onto the subject of Soviet genocide. Let's quickly shift back before our accountant's grandmother bursts into tears.

Too many businesses operate from a position of weakness and appeasement. When a new hire makes a mistake, he or she is given another shot. Fine. But frequently that new employee keeps getting shot after shot, no matter how many times the same mistake occurs. No one likes to fire people (except for the guy at our office we use to fire people—that dude loves it!). And certainly no one likes to get fired. But sometimes identifying a wrong fit at the workplace and dealing with it right away is in the best interests of everyone involved.

On a larger corporate scale, it boggles our minds how often wildly overpaid executives completely screw up . . . and then are rewarded with another opportunity to make the same mistake. Often these second chances are accompanied by pay hikes and fancier titles. This should never be tolerated. Aside from the lasting damage caused by coddling and promoting the error-prone, it threatens the very fabric of the American family. Because when our minds are boggled, we become angry, distracted, and emotionally unavailable, and then our kids suffer.

So before you rehire that caterer who gave everyone salmonella at the office Christmas party and before you offer additional stock options to the CEO who's driving your company into the toilet, think of our children. Also think of the following examples.

strange bedfellow

When we say "politics," what do you think of? If your answer is "Brave men and women who selflessly sacrifice their time and efforts to make this great nation of ours even greater," then you have been exposed to near lethal doses of chemical solvents and should check yourself into a hospital with a good Hazmat unit immediately. If your answer is "Venal, self-serving creeps whose morals would embarrass Satan," then you're our kind of people. And we have a story to tell you about politics and one politician in particular. Like all good political stories, this one starts in Washington, D.C. Actually, it starts in Mississippi, but it doesn't get good until it hits Washington.

Once upon a time there a little boy named Marion Shepilov Barry, Jr. He was a gifted student, a tireless fighter for civil rights, and in 1974 he became a politician. Some of his early career highlights include receiving a master's degree in organic chemistry, serving as president of the Washington, D.C., school board, and getting shot by radical Muslim terrorists.

With sparkling credentials like that, it's no surprise that Marion became mayor of D.C. He served with distinction and was reelected three times. Sure, there were some nagging rumors of drug use, but there's always mudslinging in any electoral process.

In 1990 the slung mud finally stuck. Marion Barry was arrested for possession of cocaine. At the time of his arrest, he was in a seedy motel with a woman who was conspicuously not his wife. He made reference to this woman in one of his famous quotations: "Bitch set me up!" This *bon mot* is right up there with some of his other legendary utterances including: "If you take out the killings, Washington actually has a very, very low crime rate," and "First, it was not a strip bar—it was an erotic club. And, second, what can I say? I'm a night owl."

Well, the owl had his wings clipped and spent six months of nights and days hooting from a perch in prison. Okay, he had made a mistake, but people make mistakes, right? Upon leaving prison, he decided to test the validity of that most compassionate of Sacred Cows, Everybody Deserves A Second Chance.

In 1992 Marion Barry won a council seat running with the slogan "He may not be perfect, but he's perfect for D.C." Drug charges notwithstanding, you've got to admire the guy's style. Two years later, he became mayor again.

Did Hizzoner Deserve this Second Chance? Judge for yourself. In 2002, police found small amounts of marijuana and cocaine in Mr. Barry's car. In 2005, the ex-mayor pleaded guilty to misdemeanor charges levied by the IRS. And, as a result of that guilty plea, he was tested for drugs. The tests revealed that he had cocaine and marijuana in his system.

We would never cast aspersions on anyone's character. That's simply not the way we roll. But without wanting to sound negative or judgmental in any way, we must conclude that Marion Barry may well be history's most compelling argument against randomly giving everyone a Second Chance.

By the way, throughout his legal, financial, and pharmaceutical difficulties, Mr. Barry has continued to serve on the Washington, D.C., city council. The fact that he has received Second Chance after Second Chance may sound surprising, but there's a simple explanation. As Marion once pointed out, "I am a great mayor; I am an upstanding Christian man; I am an intelligent man; I am a deeply educated man; I am a humble man."

cable guy

Gerald Levin is, by all traditional methods of tallying success, a very successful man. That is to say, he's rich. He has been the CEO of HBO, Time Warner, and AOL Time Warner. He's also on the board of a million board things and probably has a very lovely apartment. All of that notwithstanding, Mr. Levin has made at least one monumental business blunder.

After the dust settled, the same people who got screwed over in the monumental blunder gave him a Second Chance. He rewarded their confidence with another, even more monumental business blunder. If we had messed up twice like that, we'd now be living in a Styrofoam geodesic dome under a freeway overpass talking to our dog and wondering where it all went wrong. In big business, however, it seems like the head honcho always comes out smelling like a rose. But we're here to remind you that, like the visionaries in Poison once sang, every rose has its thorn.

Back in the early '90s, Gerald Levin was at the forefront of a technological revolution. He saw a day when TV viewers would have a totally interactive relationship with their sets. People could shop, read, learn, and do business all through their televisions. Mr. Levin was so confident in the inevitability and profitability of this impending breakthrough that he dedicated a tremendous amount of Time Warner's resources toward its development.

In 1995, Levin was finally ready to test his brave new vision of the future. The Full Service Network was launched in Orlando, Florida. It was a total and unmitigated disaster. Time Warner took a bath financially. The company and Mr. Levin were made to look ridiculous. For reasons that elude us, Mr.

Levin wasn't fired, reprimanded, or made to stand in a corner wearing a pointy hat. Instead he was allowed to continue to pilot Time Warner's (leaky) ship of state.

Sixteen years later, Gerald approved a more than $160 billion merger between Time Warner and AOL. This was the big one—the move that was going to show the world that the company's confidence in Gerald Levin was well founded.

The merger was another unmitigated disaster. Within two years the newly merged megacompany was worth 75% less than it had been. They were burdened by massive debt and had to write off billions in assets.

Levin, meanwhile, retired early. He cashed out big-time and left everyone else at the company holding the bag. The bag, unfortunately, was filled with lame ideas, corporate corrosion, and chipped marbles.

Either Carlos Castaneda or Erik Estrada once said that "those who do not remember the past are condemned to repeat it." Carlos (or Erik) clearly didn't work for Time Warner. Sometimes, even if the past is remembered, they still let you repeat it. And repeat it and repeat it until our cable bills are through the roof.

Internal Competition
Leads To Better Results

When we were younger, we thought that "internal competition" referred to some kind of intrathoracic rivalry between the heart and the lungs. Now that we're older we realize that when we were younger, we were stupid. We also realize that "internal competition" refers to a corporate strategy that is single-handedly responsible for half of the world's Maalox and Kaopectate sales.

Pitting fellow workers against one another has become standard operating procedure. It may seem a little *Lord of the Flies*-y, but many bosses, managers, and business school professors insist that Internal Competition Leads To Better Results. The theory behind it is that by applying pressure to your resources, you can force out the best of what they have to offer—kind of like making diamonds . . . or squeezing toothpaste.

The proponents of this gladiatorial business philosophy tend to be aggressive, hyperconfident, type-A personalities. The kind of people who would excel if you pitted them against their coworkers. In many cases, the application of this philosophy has clearly led to corporate success. In particular, we see significant, short-term gains in companies where employees are in a constant struggle with one another to impress their way up the food chain.

We feel that the long-term benefits of this outlook are

limited, however. Being in constant fear for your survival at work may spur you to push yourself harder than you have before. And you may achieve results. But what happens when you start hating the very feeling of approaching your office? What kind of results will you achieve then? How productive will you be when you're nervous and angry and totally stressed out all the time? And, most important, how healthy will the company be when it can no longer count on its employees to support one another?

For the answers to these and other pressing questions, let's go to the mall.

superstore

People who like to think of themselves as sophisticated and worldly often decry the omnipresence of the American mall. They snootily assert that we have lost any sense of regionalism and uniqueness because, wherever you go, you find the same fourteen branded uber-businesses occupying the same mammoth warehouse-sized stores in the middle of the same nondescript malls. These people are pedants and snobs and our print production manager's mother-in-law. They might be interested to discover that, throughout Europe—that paragon of sophistication, worldliness, and regional identity—one finds very similar giant chain stores standing sentry over very similar malls. The only difference is that in Europe the cavernous furniture wholesaler is just a five-minute drive from some dusty Carolingian ruins. Big whoop.

This is all a long-winded, roundabout way of saying that we don't blame CompUSA for the death of indigenous American culture. We do, however, blame CompUSA for a lot of other stuff. They were never able to fix our Toshiba desktop back in 1997, essentially driving us into the arms of the nearest Mac. And they believed way too much in the efficacy of that silly Sacred Cow, Internal Competition Leads To Better Results.

James Halpin used to be the CEO of CompUSA. During his tenure he often bragged that he had instilled a high-performance work culture at the company. The key component to this high-performance work culture was Halpin's assertion that "you should consider your coworker your competition."

Halpin reinforced this decree at every opportunity. During quarterly meetings of his twenty regional managers, he would draw a line down the middle of the table. He would seat the top ten performers behind the line. He placed the bottom ten performers in front of the line next to the senior team because, as he insisted, "They have to listen to everything we've got to say."

He would also force the underperforming managers to wear tags with their "shrink numbers" (totals of lost or stolen inventory from their stores). Halpin believed that by publicizing lousy results and shaming less successful employees publicly, he was creating an atmosphere wherein everyone would always try their hardest.

Looking back, it's surprising that Halpin never demanded that his workers sing the CompUSA fight song in their underwear while wrestling in Crisco and downing Jell-O shots. His methodology has the stale beer and putrefying popcorn reek of the frat house. And we all know what productive workers drunken frat boys are.

Initially, Halpin's combative technique pushed everyone to work harder. But pretty soon it just burned out most of his employees. The ones at the bottom of the barrel felt exhausted, belittled, and unappreciated. The ones at the top of the heap worried constantly that it could all be taken away in an instant.

The successful employees were actually disincentivized from helping their struggling coworkers. Why would a top-ten manager lend a hand to a bottom-ten manager? For all he knew, next quarter he might end up "below the line" with the losers, getting yelled at and humiliated.

Not surprisingly, CompUSA ran into serious financial trouble around this time. They had a variety of systemic problems. Their chain-wide management structure was splintered and redundant. They invested money and resources into new product development before the machinery was in place to make those new products. And, somewhat surprisingly for "the computer superstore," their computer system was archaic and unreliable. So Halpin's constant fomenting of Internal Competition wasn't the only reason that CompUSA hit the skids. But the fact that, thanks to James Halpin, corporate morale was horrendous certainly didn't help.

In 1997, "the Street" put CompUSA's value at $3.5 billion. In 2000, a Mexican investment group bought the company for $500 million. Needless to say, one of their first moves was to fire James Halpin.

superstars

If there's one place where competition should always be encouraged, it's sports. After all, isn't sports synonymous with competition? Isn't it? Maybe not, huh? Well, there's some connection there. Maybe they're homonyms. No? What are homonyms anyway? Are they like hominy grits? And what are hominy grits? Wow, we could do this all day, but it's getting late and we're starting to smell burnt toast and almond blossoms. The point we're tying to make is that competition and sports are fundamentally intertwined. So logic would dictate that in the sports world, Internal Competition should definitely Lead To Better Results. But that's not always the case.

There are many different kinds of internal competition. Three guys fighting it out in spring training to become the team's starting third baseman is a healthy form of internal competition. You've got to structure things that way or you might wind up with Wilson Betamit playing third and Alex Rodriguez riding the bench all season long. And, regardless of A-Rod's postseason inconsistencies, that substitution just ain't gonna fly.

Head-to-head battles are one form of friction that a lot of managers count on to make sure they're fielding the best team possible (this is both a sports reference and a sports-y business analogy). But pay structure is another tool used to stimulate internal competition—and this tool isn't as effective. Major League Baseball is a lot like many other big businesses. One of the ways the bosses reward their stars is by paying them a great deal of money. This is supposed to achieve two goals: 1) it keeps the stars happy, and 2) it encourages the lesser players to work harder in order to someday achieve massive paydays of their own.

GE, Lincoln, and Microsoft all reward their top performers at exponentially higher rates than the rest of the staff. Major League Baseball operates along a similar line. Most teams have one or two superstars with insanely inflated salaries and then a supporting cast who make a lot but nothing compared with the Big Boys. GE, Lincoln, and Microsoft have all thrived within this system. A 1999 study, however, suggests that baseball may be struggling with it.

Matt Bloom, a business professor from Notre Dame, studied twenty-nine baseball teams over an eight-year period. He discovered that teams with wide payroll gaps between their highest and lowest paid players had significantly worse won-loss records than teams with narrower gaps. What this means is that Matt Bloom has a ton of free time on his hands. It also means that traditional beliefs about the value of internal competition may be in dire need of readjustment.

As well as the highly paid superstars played, they couldn't make up for the flagging play of their underpaid teammates. And the more underpaid the teammates perceived themselves to be, the worse they played. Teams where there was greater salary equity between players performed better as a team. Bloom's study implies that companies like GE, Lincoln, and Microsoft may be succeeding *in spite* of the inequities of their pay structure.

We're not suggesting that the cure to what ails the worlds of business and sports is institutional socialism. Those guys believed in nothing but Sacred Cows and, if you ever tried to point that out, you'd wake up in Siberia with a bump on your head and a bowl of moldy borscht in your lap. Besides, we know we could beat the Cuban baseball team if we played at a neutral site and our best pitchers weren't busy hunting elk in the off-season. We're just shining a light on the ineffectiveness of certain revered business practices. Internal Competition doesn't always Lead To Better Results. Sometimes it just leads to the San Francisco Giants.

The Gate Strikes Back:
Five Sacred Cows Of Advertising

3. *"Advertising is a science, like engineering, with
some incidental esthetic potential."*
—Rosser Reeves

Rosser Reeves was an advertising guru who pioneered the development of television commercials and used his love of science to discover that the milk chocolate of M&M's "melts in your mouth, not in your hands." Frankly, we've always felt that this slogan is somewhat duplicitous. Of course the chocolate doesn't melt in your hands, but that freaking candy coating sure does. Sneaky devil, that Rosser Reeves. Not that we should be surprised. He did, after all, use doctors to help advertise cigarettes. Reeves was a serious man, and he took the ad business seriously as well. His tremendous influence has led to advertising agencies still taking themselves and their products way too seriously. It's important to understand the science of the job. But artistic creativity and overall playfulness are key components to succeeding in this industry. Heck, if we wanted to be scientists, we would have become scientists.

Don't Screw Up

This is the most saucily titled of all our many chapters. And we hate to use the "S word" so brazenly, but we feel we need to make our point. Don't Screw Up is a Sacred Cow in almost every field of human endeavor. One of us was raised in a strict, old-fashioned household with a dominating patriarch who constantly exhorted his son not to Screw Up. Not surprisingly, this was also the one of us who didn't do well on his SATs, destroyed three different automobiles before he turned twenty-five, and who cries during the *opening* credits of *The Great Santini* (which he watches twice a year without fail, alone in his garage with some caramel-flavored popcorn and a box of Kleenex).

Those of us who have children know that yelling Don't Screw Up at them is a surefire way to get them to Screw Up all the time. That knowledge, however, isn't sufficient enough to prevent us from yelling Don't Screw Up at our children. It's a simple, provocative thought that seems to come from a place of caring and concern but is more about fear and lack of confidence. Also, telling people not to Screw Up is an incredibly hard habit to break. The same holds true in the workplace.

You want your employees to do well. You don't want them to mess up. But if you tell them not to mess up, they mess up. Are you supposed to tell them to mess up? That doesn't work either.

What's a good manager supposed to do? If anticipating failure guarantees failure but demanding achievement also leads to failure, how do you get people to do what you want them to do? The answer is . . . we have no idea. In our experience, everyone responds to different kinds of encouragement and/or admonitions. Everything works or doesn't work depending on the situation. We have even had success in the past yelling at certain workers, "Don't Screw Up!" Sometimes that's exactly what these guys needed to hear.

The people who respond to that kind of verbal abuse, however, are few and far between. They tend to be superconfident risk-takers who regularly ride the edge. Our reminding them that there will be repercussions for their lack of fiscal or creative responsibility provides them with just enough grounding not to fly off into outer space.

These are extremely rare cases. In almost every other case, the insistence that someone not Screw Up is just a knee-jerk reaction based in fear that leads to disaster. For the most part, it's better to encourage someone to feel free to Screw Up and live with the consequences than to have them so scared of Screwing Up that they're frozen in terror and never have the chance for greatness.

Achieving the goals you set for yourself is fine. That never leads to surprises—good or bad. If you want your R&D department to come up with a lower-calorie biscuit and they know that if they Screw Up you'll fire them all, then they'll come up with a lower-calorie biscuit. But if they know that there's room for them to take some chances without getting the boot, then they'll push the envelope a little. Sure, maybe they'll accidentally burn down the factory and you'll have to move in with your parents and sell pencils for a living. But there's also a chance that, while working on those new, light biscuits, they'll accidentally discover the cure for cancer. It's not much of a chance, but you never know. Sometimes massive mistakes have led to amazing discoveries.

sweet relief

In the late 1980s, scientists at the pharmaceutical company Pfizer were interested in developing a drug to treat hypertension. Eager to stamp out the scourge of high blood pressure, they began research on a compound that would increase the activity of a molecule called atrial natriuretic peptide (ANP). They were hoping that this new twist on ANP would be the wonder drug they were searching for.

Their experiments led to the creation of a compound known as UK-92,480—possibly the only name even less catchy than atrial natriuretic peptide. After some initially encouraging results in lab and animal testing, UK-92,480 was tried out on human subjects. Unfortunately, the results showed that UK-92,480 was no more effective in treating run-of-the-mill hypertension than the placebo that had been administered.

Most scientists at this point would have thrown in the towel and moved on to other research. The good folks at Pfizer (and we use that term with tongue in cheek as we are convinced that most pharmaceutical companies have the morals of Wile E. Coyote on a crack bender) turned out not to be towel thrower–inners. Perhaps they were freethinking mavericks. Perhaps they just got lucky. Or perhaps they knew that their bosses had given them the latitude to Screw Up a little. Whatever the reason, they turned a modest failure into a mammoth success.

See, just because there was no real difference between UK-92,480 and the placebo in terms of preventing hypertension doesn't mean there were no differences at all. There was a difference. A huge difference. The male research subjects who ingested the placebo didn't all have raging erections (the UK-92,480 guys did).

If we were scientists and we entered a lab to discover that a bunch of strange men still had high blood pressure and now half of them were sporting something even higher, we would probably go running for the hills. But that's just us. We've never liked science. We like books, drawings, and high-quality, ice-cold sake. The Pfizer fellas, however, took one look at their research and said some version of "Eureka!"

Okay, so they screwed up with the hypertension medicine. But they had inadvertently stumbled across something way better. Face it, if your blood pressure isn't working properly, it's a minor inconvenience that *might* lead to death. If your penis isn't working properly, you might as well be dead. That's just a fact of life. And Pfizer recognized that fact right away.

They immediately began the process of patenting and getting approval for this new wonder drug (now technically called sildenafil citrate—another lame name). Before you could say, "Bob Dole's a wild man in the sack," Pfizer was releasing Viagra (finally, a catchy name!). And before you could say, "Isn't it funny that Rafael Palmeiro admitted to taking Viagra but lied about taking steroids?" Viagra was a multibillion-dollar juggernaut.

Nobody wanted those scientists to Screw Up. And maybe the experimental laboratory environment is more conducive to failure and learning from failure than the boardroom or the sales department. But that little blue pill can teach us all a lesson: Don't be afraid to make mistakes. And we know it's blue only because we've seen the commercials.

tax relief

Intuit Incorporated of Mountain View, California, claims to "create new ways to manage personal finances and small businesses that are so profound and simple, customers cannot imagine going back to the old way." Bold claims from a bunch of egghead CPAs. (No offense intended, of course. Some of our dearest friends are egghead CPAs. Well, actually, only our CPA is an egghead CPA, but we like him a lot.) You would think that a company whose primary function is to help individuals and corporations prepare and file tax returns would be particularly adverse to Screwing Up. After all, if you Screw Up on the operating table, the worst that can happen is the patient dies. If you Screw Up filing your taxes, you could get the federal government on your tail and that's exponentially worse than being dead.

Surprisingly, Intuit Inc. has made a variety of boneheaded mistakes in the past, and, even more surprisingly, they embrace these mistakes. Not only do they embrace them, but they go so far as to reward the perpetrators on occasion.

Their most splashy failure occurred in 2005. A team of Intuit employees decided to go after an untapped market: younger tax filers. Their logic went something like this: Young people have to file tax returns; young people like hip-hop music; if we tie our tax return products to hip-hop music, the young people will flock to us like cold sores to Kid Rock's lips. (See, we tried to appeal to the youngsters there too but failed miserably. The simile was grotesque and irrelevant—Kid Rock has got to be around fifty-three years old by now. Just forget the whole thing, okay?)

Intuit actually created a Web site called RockYourRefund. com and tried to get Generation Y to buy their products using incentives like discounts at Expedia and Best Buy. They even offered to deposit tax refunds directly onto supposedly cool Visa cards issued by wacky hip-hop mogul Russell Simmons.

Not surprisingly, the lure of Web discounts and b-boy credit cards was not enough to entice the young (but not moronic) consumers. Intuit basically didn't get any new business out of the campaign, and they just wasted a lot of money on promotion and advertising. In other words, they Screwed Up.

But instead of hiding from their errors or blaming them on someone else (both of which strategies we would have opted for), the team behind this campaign presented their company with a carefully studied analysis of the disaster. They even drew some larger conclusions from it like "Generation Y-ers aren't drawn to Web sites that feel too much like advertising," and "Having Russell Simmons's signature on a piece of plastic isn't enough to make young people not hate paying taxes."

There's no Viagra-esque miracle story here. This marketing failure didn't accidentally lead to an industry-altering new invention. The lessons learned from the failure didn't remake Intuit into a brand-new super-business. So it might appear odd that Intuit's chairman, Scott Cook, gave the hip-hop tax team an award onstage in front of two hundred people. Was Scott Cook a deranged lunatic in the throes of advanced dementia? Maybe—we don't know the guy and we weren't there for the ceremony. But a more plausible explanation can be gleaned from what Mr. Cook told his employees that night: "It's only a failure if we fail to get the learning."

Look past the crazy syntax and you'll see a guy who's not afraid to Screw Up. And it's that attitude that has helped Intuit grow and thrive. Right about now, one of us probably wishes that Scott Cook was his daddy. And he's crying all over the keyboard.

make belief

Back in 1989 Andrew Jarecki was struggling with a problem that has plagued us all, and no, it wasn't psoriasis. He was tired of racing to his local movie house, waiting in line for twenty minutes, and then discovering that the last ticket was just sold to the woman in front of him who barely speaks English and therefore won't be able to fully appreciate the subtle wordplay of *Honey, I Shrunk the Kids*. He wished that there were some way of purchasing movie tickets ahead of time, thereby guaranteeing him a seat to all kinds of horrible Rick Moranis movies.

Andrew figured that if he would pay for a service like that, probably a lot of other people would too. And that's how he invented Moviefone.

But inventing Moviefone is a lot easier than implementing Moviefone. And Andrew's first move was such a disaster that it almost killed the great idea before it got a chance to become a great idea.

The question facing Mr. Jarecki was how to turn his brilliant thought into a practical reality. His first instinct was to go with simplicity. Once he and his partners were ready to start pre-selling tickets over the phone, they worked out a deal with a Los Angeles theater. They installed a computer and a printer hooked up to a phone line via a modem in the box office of the theater. They advertised the service, telling people that they just had to call a number, give their credit card info, and their tickets to the film would be waiting in will-call envelopes at the theater.

The test film for the new service was *Terminator 2*, which turned out to be the highest grossing movie of the year. On the first day of Moviefone's operation, the theater staff opened the box office doors to discover a mass of printed envelopes sprayed all over the place. The phone orders had completely swamped Jarecki's primitive delivery system and turned *Terminator 2's* opening night into an opening nightmare. (Allow us to sit back and enjoy that witty turn of phrase as if it were a fine wine or a ripe papaya.)

The whole process of launching Moviefone had been an experiment for Mr. Jarecki and his partners. They had no way of knowing how successful the business venture might be. Their mistake in setting up such a low-tech delivery system caused some headaches for their company and for the theater. It also turned out to be the most accurate indicator of the commercial viability of Moviefone.

If one night's Moviefone receipts could almost cripple a large Los Angeles theater, then that meant that people were dying to take advantage of what they had to offer. Would this realization have been driven home so convincingly if Jarecki hadn't made the error he made? Probably not. As Mr. Jarecki once said, "Our 'mistake' also illustrated quite graphically that there was a demand for this service, and that we were the ones to handle it."

Moviefone flourished because its founders gave themselves the leeway to make mistakes and learn from them. Although, for our money, the key component to the business's success was the mellifluent voice of cofounder Russ Leatherman, better known as "Mr. Moviefone."

Create A
Corporate Culture

Everyone's always talking about Corporate Culture. Including us. We just did a quick word search through this book's computer file and we discovered that we use the phrase "Corporate Culture" 6,845 times. It's our third most commonly used phrase behind "Fiduciary Malfeasance," and "Wicker Will Be Tomorrow's Corian." So, what does Corporate Culture mean? Well, it has different definitions for different people—and therein lies the rub. And as any good barbecuer knows, the only worthwhile thing to do with rub is to vigorously apply it to some beef and throw that sucker on the grill.

Most folks would probably define Corporate Culture as a series of values and goals shared by everyone within a company. Usually this is established in a dense and convoluted mission statement. Usually this mission statement is generated by overpaid think tankers hired by the company to explain to them what their Corporate Culture should be. Usually this Corporate Culture exists solely on the sheet of paper upon which the mission statement is printed. Just because some business school pinhead tells you that your business stands for "Integrity," "Passion," "Commitment," and "Excellence" doesn't make it so. It also doesn't really mean anything. What kind of moron would announce that their business stands for "Lying," "Apathy,"

"Flightiness," and "Mediocrity"? No one would admit to that—especially now that UPN is off the air.

Corporate Culture is a very nebulous concept. Too often it defines what someone wishes their company was like, but it in no way represents what's really going on. The best definition that we've ever heard for Corporate Culture is: "What happens when management isn't looking." In other words, what's your company *really* like—at its core? When the bosses aren't cracking their whips to make sure that everyone toes some artificial company line, what's the natural state of your business?

The drive to Create this Corporate Culture can be a vital, healthy part of a growing enterprise. It can also become a stagnant and divisive force. We feel the key aspect to any Corporate Culture is the degree to which it is visionary. When Corporate Culture looks forward and points the way to where the company should be headed, that's a good thing. When Corporate Culture is totally artificial, that's a bad thing. And when your Corporate Culture becomes so limiting and rigid that it chokes the life out of your business, that's a really bad thing.

Just take a look at Al Davis (if you dare).

silver & black

We are not brave men. We're brave enough to admit that—but that's as far as our bravery goes. When we were in the fourth grade, we once hid in the boys' locker room for three and a half days to avoid a fistfight with a sixth grader. The sixth grader was much bigger than us, but in retrospect, we think we could have taken her. We didn't try, however, because, as we just said, we're not brave men. And, as such, we have no desire to incite the ire of Raider Nation.

For those of you who do not know, Raider Nation is the legion of football fans who worship the Oakland Raiders. Raider Nation has always been known as a bunch of rough, dangerous, crazy beasts who would rather rip your head off than shake your hand. And if you're foolish enough to root for the opposition, they wouldn't even be that nice. The team they support has a reputation for being even crazier and more dangerous than their fans.

The owner of the Oakland Raiders is Al Davis. He has the grizzled skin of a six-hundred-year-old man, the feathery pompadour of Louis XIV on a windy day, and the toughness and strength of a gladiator in his prime. He likes wearing jumpsuits. He is a badass. A long time ago he built a football team in his likeness, and he has overseen all things Raiders ever since.

Al Davis believes in Corporate Culture. And with the Oakland Raiders, the Corporate Culture has always been very clear: Hit hard, hit often, and go deep. Al is famous for saying "Just win, baby!" and for announcing that the key to the Raiders is the vertical game. As far as the Big Boss is concerned, the Oakland Raiders are all about firing the ball downfield. He has always hired mean, hard-hitting defensive players and tall, fast receivers. This philosophy has led to success. The Raiders have won three Super Bowls. The only problem is . . . now the Raiders stink. (Please don't hurt us, Raider Nation.)

The Raiders' slogan is "Commitment to Excellence." Unfortunately, they may have to replace that with "Commitment to Sucking." One of the main reasons that the Raiders stink is their Corporate Culture. The organization has steadfastly remained committed to its founding principles. The only problem is, they no longer have the personnel or the coaching staff to successfully hit hard, hit often, and (especially) go deep.

Their offensive line is porous so their quarterbacks don't get good protection. Their quarterbacks aren't particularly good, though, so even if they did have more protection, they still couldn't necessarily get the ball downfield. And their receivers are either disgruntled and refuse to play or they're disgruntled and injured. Being disgruntled used to be a source of pride for all Raider employees. Now it's just what you feel before demanding a contract renegotiation or a trade.

Al Davis has forced the present and future of his business to comply with a Corporate Culture rooted in the past. The Raiders always hired troublesome malcontents and it worked for them. Fred Biletnikoff, Mike Haynes, and (especially) the loathsome Bill Romanowski were classic Raiders who were perpetually on the verge of complete mental collapse but whose deviant lunacy crushed the opposition and brought victories. The team still has plenty of head cases, only now they're not bringing results—just headaches. The Raiders have always thought pass first, run second. They still think that way, only now their passing game stinks *and* they have no running game.

Another team might be able to squeeze out more wins from this bunch by changing their offensive philosophy—by not being constrained by their Corporate Culture. But that's not permissible with the Raiders. Raiders play Raider football no matter what.

There's a small company out there called InsureMe that helps customers find the cheapest insurance to suit their needs. They have a Corporate Culture that works for them. It's based on an incredibly simple premise, "Do the right thing." That's it. The quality that the CEO has chosen to define every element of his business is the overwhelming desire to "Do the right thing." That allows for an environment of change and growth. If InsureMe owned the Raiders, they would be able to adapt to

the changes in personnel and competition, an
would be regular fixtures in the postseason.

However, instead of embracing a Corporate C
ways looks forward for new ways to achieve, ₁
doomed Raider Nation to a very depressing foot
experience—probably for years to come. And that
for all of us, because Raider Nation is tough to deal
they're in a good mood. When they're surly, heed ₍
Hide in the locker room for as long as it takes.

blue

The following is an excerpt from a large corporation's c₍
mission statement:

> The companies that can create a culture of innovation
> are the companies that will succeed in the next era of
> business. . . . That culture is defined by its ability to an-
> ticipate customer needs and market dynamics, then
> quickly respond to meet those challenges.

As far as mission statements go, we give this one a solid B. It's
just dry and dull enough not to scare the old folks, but it suggests sufficient progressiveness and forethought to entice the
youngsters. There are only two qualities to this statement that
make it truly surprising: 1) The corporation in question is IBM,
and 2) they actually seem to be following their own advice.

As far as we're concerned, IBM has always been one of the best
examples of why Creating a Corporate Culture can be a big mistake. When you close your eyes, bite your lip, and think of IBM,
what do you see? Big Blue, right? Suits and ties. Middle-aged

ite men in fedoras carrying thick briefcases to meetings with
her middle-aged white men in fedoras carrying thick brief-
ses. A computer chip. Honestly—that's what we think of and
that order. And there's good reason for it.

Almost since its inception, IBM has worked hard to create
nd maintain a Corporate Culture that was all about serious,
conservative, traditional, buttoned-down American Business.
For a company based on technology and innovation, the image
that they have always tried to convey has never been particularly
innovative. It's almost as if they thought the whole "cutting edge
thing" might scare people away, so they worked hard to appear
as staid and Eisenhower-y as possible.

This was probably a successful plan . . . back when Eisenhower was president. The changing world of technology, computers, and automated office machinery must have been
perceived as strange and threatening to IBM's customers in the
distant past. But creating a Corporate Culture of somber re-
spectability and glacier-paced advancement never allowed IBM
to change with the times.

As suspicion of and distrust for new technology was replaced
in the popular consciousness by excitement and anticipation,
IBM kept on presenting themselves as Big Blue—you know,
your grandfather's computer company. New product development lagged and sales became sluggish. They were becoming
victims of their own painstakingly created Corporate Culture.
Obviously IBM was still a massive concern that generated huge
revenues. But their size was becoming unwieldy and their rev-
enue margins weren't as healthy as they used to be. Both elements pointed to a potentially unsteady future—and IBM was
supposedly all about steadiness and dependability.

They finally woke up and smelled the digital coffee around
2003. They began a company-wide shift in their concept of

their own Corporate Culture. Suddenly, the company that used to make conservative dress code demands of their entire workforce was spearheading corporation-wide Internet Jams. Unfortunately, this doesn't mean they were orchestrating mass air guitar and karaoke sessions. The Jams were online discussions conducted among all IBM personnel in an attempt to redefine the Culture and attitudes of the company. They even used high-tech software to identify themes in the tens of thousands of responses and then addressed those themes in their new vision of themselves.

Don't get us wrong—if you're some kind of insane computer genius with face tattoos and eyeball piercings who wants to surf your experimental hovercraft to work and crank out the speed metal while you write code, IBM probably still isn't the place for you. But they have done an admirable job of adjusting what was a stifling, limiting Corporate Culture to adapt to the bold new world that psychos like you have foisted on the rest of us.

The Customer
Is Always Right

We know what you're thinking. You're thinking, "Stop right there. 'The Customer Is Always Right' is a Sacred Cow I actually believe in. Please don't kill it. In fact, if you do kill it, you might as well kill me too." Relax. We're not killing anybody. We're sweet, gentle folk who are meek as baby lambs. Also we're on probation and we ain't going back to the hole.

Look, we're not saying the customer is always wrong. We're not even saying the customer is usually wrong. We're just saying that slavishly kowtowing to the idea that the customer is the ultimate authority on how your business should operate is a surefire way to wind up with an inoperable business.

Hey, we're customers too. And, if you're anything like us, you probably are right. A lot of the time. Maybe most of the time. Just not *always*. "Always" is bad, remember? Even the movie *Always* was bad. One of Spielberg's only total bombs. Richard Dreyfuss and Audrey Hepburn? What kind of insane casting is that?

The Customer Is Always Right is one of those Sacred Cows that just sounds good when you hear it. That's the way businesses should be run. Treat the clients with respect. Give them what they want and be polite about it. Sure. That's a damn fine theory, and when it works, it works great. But what happens when the customer simply doesn't want what you're selling? Are they still right? 'Cause if they are, you might as well shove all your stuff in a cardboard box, hand in your parking pass, and head home. If the customer is always right and the customer thinks your widgets suck, then you're out of the widget business, right? Well . . . probably. But sometimes great successes have been spawned from the fervent belief that the customer has no idea what he or she is talking about. As Henry Ford once said, "If I'd asked the consumer what they wanted, they would have said a faster horse."

In 1946, when Dr. Benjamin Spock published *The Common Sense Book of Baby and Child Care*, his average customer was totally clueless. He didn't assume that they were right. He assumed that they were putting diapers on their kids' heads. He had confidence in his own rightness and in the importance of properly educating his customers.

But there's another more subtle level at which believing the Customer Is Always Right can be problematic. Focusing exclusively on the wonderfulness of your customers can alienate and demoralize your employees. Without a happy and motivated workforce, your business will wither and die. And then you'll feel really stupid for wasting all that time brownnosing your customers, who are now buying widgets across the street. Here are two probative examples that we siphoned out of the Universal Consciousness with a gold-plated Krazy Straw. Enjoy!

meat and potatoes

HCL Technologies is one of those companies that completely baffle us. No matter how many times we read their informational brochure, corporate profile, or mission statement, we simply do not understand what they do. Apparently it has something to do with technology and digital something or other. But we don't know if that's, like, digital cameras or if they make those paintings that look like photographs from far away but when you get real close they just look like a bunch of dots. Or maybe they do something else altogether. We simply can't figure it out. It's a mystery that can only be solved by people smarter than us (in other words: pretty much anyone else).

What we do know is that HCL Technologies started out thirty years ago in a garage and now generates annual revenues of over 3.5 billion dollars. Whatever they're doing, they're doing it a lot and really well.

We also know that HCL attributes a great deal of its success to a relatively new corporate policy: "People first, customers second." (For a company that could buy and sell Guam, they're a little fuzzy with their corporate lingo. By "people," they mean their employees. They're not trying to imply that their customers aren't people.)

Anyway, "People first, customers second" was meant to put HCL's staff (all 40,000 of them) at the forefront of company strategy. It also helped create a real sense of managerial accountability. Everyone who works for HCL has access to an interactive computer forum wherein they can ask questions and make suggestions to management. Surprisingly, they don't seem to use this option to tell management to drop dead and/or to create dirty limericks. Management routinely sends out employee opinion polls to gauge interest in and support for new policies and initiatives (and dirty limericks).

The company has instituted an appraisal system in which everyone has equal say in grading the performance of their underlings, fellow workers, and bosses. They have also introduced something called "electronic trouble tickets." If any employee has an issue at work, they file an electronic complaint. The company then grades itself on the speed with which that complaint gets resolved to everyone's satisfaction. We once filed an Internet complaint with a certain ice cream conglomerate who shall remain nameless because our pint of dulce de leche didn't have enough caramel in it. We have yet to hear back from them. But the guys at HCL have come up with a more effective system than the anonymous ice cream company (hint: it rhymes with Flagen Blaz).

HCL does not have a corporate policy of being rude to their customers. They don't make fun of their customers' garish neckties or sagging butts. In fact, being polite and solicitous to their customers is an important part of their business (whatever the hell that is). HCL just realized that making sure that their employees are feeling content and invested in the process is their first and most important job. Apparently they were right. The revenues of their incomprehensible mystery business have more than septupled over the last six years.

tuna carpaccio

If you woke one morning with a sudden, desperate hankering for a ramekin filled with fig and walnut *crostata*, your options would be limited. You could 1) drink a mug of NyQuil and go back to sleep, 2) have some oatmeal and let your dreams die, or 3) immediately go to one of Danny Meyer's many New York City restaurants.

Danny Meyer is to dining out what Elvis Presley is to houseboat. Wait. That makes absolutely no sense. No wonder we scored so poorly on our SATs. What we mean to say is that Danny Meyer owns and operates some of the finest restaurants in New York. They're the kinds of places where people (that is to say, idiots) wait for months just to get a reservation. (We have a policy about waiting for food or movies—we don't do it. Nothing's so delicious or exciting that it can't be put off until another, less crowded moment.) Fortunately for Danny Meyer, however, the fifty billion people living in and around New York City don't agree. His restaurants all serve excellent food and they are all crowded—always.

Recently Mr. Meyer published a book called *Setting the Table: The Transforming Power of Hospitality in Business*. So, the guy has actually written the book on hospitality. If anyone anywhere ever believed in the Sacred Cow of The Customer Is Always Right, it has to be him, right? No, sir, ma'am, or small child.

Danny certainly believes in treating the customer well. He has achieved tremendous success by making the rich and famous feel comfortable while making the average patron feel rich and famous. He just happens to think that the customer comes second and that his employees are the most important part of his business. In the *Wall Street Journal* he once said, "I do not believe that the customer is always right. I do believe it is good business to always give the customer the opportunity to be heard." And in an article in *Time* magazine he said, "If you are devoted to your staff and can promise them much more than a paycheck, something to believe in, you will then get the best service for your customers."

Unlike HCL, we know exactly what Danny Meyer does. He makes orange-fennel osso buco and ratatouille-stuffed zucchini blossoms. Well, he doesn't make them; his chefs make them. But he greenlights everything. HCL is an ultra-business-y international conglomerate generating billions. Danny Meyer is a trim dude with graying hair who generates some wicked-good blueberry-lemon meringue pie. But they have both come up with a similar solution for success: Sometimes the customer is right; sometimes the customer is wrong. But if your employees are happy, you have a much better chance of seeing that customer again.

salted peanuts

There are some who say that man was not meant to fly. They feel that if God/The Supreme Being/Oprah Winfrey meant for us to take to the skies, He/It/She would have blessed us with wings. We are of the opinion, however, that air travel is a good thing, because if you really want to get to Maui, floating on an inner tube is simply not an effective means of transportation.

Herb Kelleher and Gordon Bethune are on our side in this argument. Herb is the CEO of Southwest and Gordon runs Continental. Southwest has been a major success since its inception, and Bethune is renowned for guiding Continental from worst to first. Both men agree on one essential business philosophy: The Customer Is Not Always Right.

Keeping their customers happy is one of the primary goals of any airline. It's right up there with keeping the planes in the sky and making sure that the in-flight magazines are unbelievably boring. But Continental and Southwest know that without happy employees who feel supported and protected by management, they'd have no planes, no customers, and no dull-but-glossy periodicals.

Bethune has said, "When we run into customers that we can't reel back in, our loyalty is with our employees. You can't treat your employees like serfs. You have to value them. If they think that you won't support them when a customer is out of line, even the smallest problem can cause resentment."

And over at Southwest there is a famous case of the Customer Not Always Being Right. One frequent traveler began a constant letter-writing campaign complaining about everything and anything. She didn't like the way they assigned seats. She didn't like that there was no first class. She missed her in-flight meal. She thought the attitude was too casual. In short, she was complaining about the very essence of Southwest Airlines.

After a lengthy back-and-forth, her complaints were kicked all the way up the ladder to Herb Kelleher's office. Herb read what she had to say and quickly sent her the following note: "Dear Mrs. Crabapple, We will miss you. Love, Herb."

Herb had confidence in his employees and in the product they offered as a team. He not only realized that this Customer Wasn't Always Right but booted her right out the door. And there was probably a happy traveler just behind her thrilled to be plucked from the purgatory of standby.

Branding
Is Expensive

Branding is an intangible but essential component of any business. Not to be confused with traditional cattle branding, business branding rarely requires the use of white-hot pig iron and, if done properly, shouldn't produce the stench of burning flesh. It should produce an easily recognizable corporate identity and encourage consumer identification and loyalty. Think "The Golden Arches," "The Macintosh Apple," "The Nike Swoosh," or "Dr. Phil's Gleaming Dome." When your product or services are instantly recognizable by a word or an image, then you've been branded and you're on your way to superstardom, mega-riches, and some scalp polish.

When it comes to branding, there are two universal truths: Everyone wants it; no one can afford it. The prevailing wisdom is that creating an instantly recognizable brand, while desperately sought after, is a prohibitively expensive proposition. We're here to tell you that the prevailing wisdom is poppycock. We repeat: Poppycock! Yes—it should be the goal of every business to establish a powerful and evocative brand. But, no—the process of establishing that brand doesn't have to break the bank.

There is an important distinction to make at this point between "branding" (verb) and "a brand" (noun). The verb version is the glitz and the marketing and the hullabaloo (for all our readers over the age of ninety). The noun form is the essence of what all companies should strive for: the creation of a corporate identity, the evocation of an emotional response when your product or services are mentioned or seen. Any company can attempt to act like a brand without spending a dime. To do this, you simply need to define your products and services in a way that makes you stand out and then align everything within your company behind that definition. The next step most companies usually lust after is making that brand universally acknowledged—that's the branding part. Too many businesses abandon the attempt to act like a brand because they're scared that the branding phase will be prohibitively expensive. This is a mistake perhaps even more foolish than allowing Whoopi Goldberg to host the Oscars (twice). She is just not funny...at all.

Obviously, branding can be expensive. And we're not going to lie to you—(Actually, we are going to lie to you—we just won't tell you when we're lying to you so you'll have to figure it out on a case by case basis. This, however, is not a case where we're lying. Honest.)—sometimes spending a lot of money is the best way to quickly and effectively spread the word that you are a brand worthy of notice. Nike, for example, is one of the world's most famous companies whose "swoosh" is revered in every house, hut, tent, tipi, yurt, igloo, chalet, troglodyte cave, and tiki bar on the planet. In order to garner this kind of acceptance, Nike has spent a fortune. Michael Jordan alone received enough money from Nike to fund his own fully operational continent. And they pay Tiger Woods enough to buy Michael Jordan's continent and ship it to Uranus.

So the word on the street has some validity—branding can be very expensive. But don't hold back out of fear of the cost. We're here to tell you to fear incredibly muscular lunatics wearing tinfoil hats. We're here to tell you to fear any and all products containing aspartame. We're here to tell you to fear clowns.

We're also here to tell you that branding doesn't have to be expensive. Just make sure to be a brand before you waste your time with all that branding. Because if you really have something original to sell, we can show you some examples of cheap but successful branding.

superman

Before we delve into this stirring tale of bravery, bicycles, and balls, there's something we need to clear up. There never has been, and there never will be, a tougher, stronger, manlier man than Lance Armstrong. We are not cyclists. We are not Texans. We never even liked Sheryl Crow. But if you or anyone else ever suggests that Lance Armstrong is guilty of doping, then we're gonna fight. If you even suggest that Lance Armstrong took one too many baby aspirin, we're gonna throw down. Because the man was given like a 2% chance of survival after they discovered metastasized cancer in his testicles, lungs, abdomen, and brain . . . and then he won the frigging Tour de France seven times in a row! We once tried to drive that course in a rented Renault and it was exhausting. He did it over and over again on a bike wearing nothing but a skintight shirt and short shorts. The man's not on steroids—he's just from the planet Krypton.

Lance Armstrong has had a profound effect on our culture. He actually managed to make riding a bicycle seem cool. He made cancer seem beatable. And he made wearing brightly colored neoprene bracelets an omnipresent fashion choice.

Before Lance and his brilliant yellow Livestrong bracelets, rubber bands were primarily used to hold together spears of broccoli. But in 2004 all that changed. The Lance Armstrong Foundation wanted to raise money for cancer research, to raise cancer awareness, and to encourage people to live life to the fullest. Together with Nike, Lance developed this simple accessory. The item cost pennies to manufacture, and it received no marketing or publicity. Lance just put it on his wrist and hit the road.

Clearly many other people out there share the same man-love that we feel for Mr. Armstrong. Because, as soon as they found out what the yellow band on Lance's wrist was all about, a bunch of his fellow cyclists started wearing them too. Then highly visible celebrities like Matt Damon and Katie Couric got into the act as well. Arguably the only smart move that John Kerry made in 2004 was to sport a Livestrong gel band.

Nike is a marketing machine. They have no qualms whatsoever about spending millions to brand a product. But no one spent much of anything on the Livestrong bracelets. They were a great product for a great cause represented by a great guy. They flew off the shelves. Not literally, obviously. Only Lance Armstrong can literally fly—and he has the good taste to do it when nobody is looking so as not to embarrass anyone. But the success of Livestrong was a true branding phenomenon.

The Lance Armstrong Foundation's initial goal was to raise five million dollars by selling the bracelets at a dollar apiece. At the time, that goal was considered extremely lofty. They probably would have been thrilled with half that amount. Since 2004 they have sold over seventy million bracelets. Lance Armstong can leap tall buildings in a single bound. Admit it, or we're going to Indian-wrestle you into submission.

rodent man

Brian Burton is not a world-class athlete like Lance Armstrong. He has no extraterrestrial super powers that we know of. But he has way better taste in music. More commonly known as Danger Mouse, Burton is an almost ubiquitous presence in pop music today (and that includes hip-hop, alt rock, and whatever the hell other genres you want to lump in with pop). He is a producer, writer, and performer currently involved in a million projects including his most visible forum, the band Gnarls Barkley.

In a lengthy article in the *New York Times*, Burton/Mouse outlined his musical philosophy. It's kind of dense and multifaceted and, frankly, at times a little bizarre and hard to understand. This is a man, after all, who never performs (and refuses to be photographed) unless he's wearing an outlandish costume. These getups include an Obi-Wan Kenobi cape, a chef's outfit, and a full-body Pink Panther suit. (Danger Mouse is the kind of eccentric genius that our dear, dear friend Robert DeNiro, would refer to as "a wackadoo." We have never met Robert DeNiro.)

In a nutshell, Burton essentially hears music in his head and then does his best to re-create it in real life. Sometimes his medium is his own band; sometimes he realizes this vision by producing other bands. But he has a very clear sound in mind—he has defined what he wants to achieve and it's completely unique. In other words, in all his musical endeavors he acts like a brand. When Danger Mouse is attached to a project, there's a particular set of expectations listeners take with them before they've even heard a note. There's an expectation of complete originality, nuanced complexity, and a little bit of funk to everything Burton does.

That's the brand. He created it by working hard and by being born a musical genius wackadoo. And that didn't cost him a penny. But how did the branding of Danger Mouse come about? How did he achieve fame and instant recognition? What did he do to achieve one million downloads of his songs in a single day? That must have cost him a fortune.

How about a couple hundred bucks?

The breadth of Danger Mouse's fame—his branding, if you will—was the result of a single event. In 2004 he was cleaning up his apartment while listening to The Beatles' *White Album*. As he listened and put away his copy of Jay-Z's *Black Album*, he had an idea. "I wonder if I could create a song only using samples from *The Black Album* and *The White Album*?" If we had this idea, we would check our foreheads for fever and finish cleaning up. Danger Mouse sat down at his computer and started working on it.

After twenty days of twelve to thirteen hours of work each day, Danger Mouse created an entire album of songs that were nothing but digital fusions of Jay-Z's *Black Album* and The Beatles' *White Album*. He made three hundred copies (there's the total cost of the project) and sent them to a bunch of friends and colleagues who he thought might be impressed by this weird intellectual/artistic endeavor he had undertaken.

They were more than impressed. Pretty soon copies of the CD (now known as *The Grey Album*) were all over the place. Everyone was talking about it, copying it, and downloading it. EMI, who owned the Beatles catalogue, heard about it and sued Danger Mouse and threatened to sue everyone who was downloading this unlicensed music.

The whole thing grew into an enormous poop storm as the album got more and more popular. An Internet group staged a protest against EMI and encouraged people to download *The Grey Album* all on the same day (known as "Grey Tuesday" in wackadoo Internet circles). That's the day that Danger Mouse tunes were downloaded one million times and he crossed over into superstardom.

The guy and his nutty musical gestalt were suddenly on the front burner of the pop consciousness. His branding was complete. And the reason it happened was because he was talented, hardworking, and incredibly lucky. But he was also ready for his branding because he had already been acting like a brand. Danger Mouse had something unique to sell to the world. Once they all saw what he was about, they bought it.

So go ahead and be a brand. Don't worry so much about the cost of branding. Take a shot and maybe things will work out for you as they did for Brian Burton. Of course it helps if you can write a song like Gnarls Barkley's "Crazy." Listen to that evil sucker once and we defy you to stop it from circling your brain forever like a dead goldfish that refuses to be flushed. Cheers!

Don't Offend Anyone

One hundred years ago, businesspeople did not worry about offending the public. They churned out their sexist cleaning products featuring the faces of smiling mothers and racist piggy banks featuring the faces of smiling slaves and never entertained the possibility that someone might be upset by these items. Or, if they did entertain the possibility, they certainly didn't care. As long as sales were strong, whether or not someone's feelings got hurt wasn't an issue.

Times have changed, however. We now have newfangled self-winding watches and we hear tell the telegraph machine is a-coming, by gum! We also have a more finely developed sense of business ethics. Selling sexist cleaning products or racist piggy banks wouldn't just be bad business today; it would be morally and ethically wrong. And that's a good thing. The fact that businesses now make a concerted effort not to hurt people, both physically and emotionally, is a huge and positive step. They used to put cocaine in Coca-Cola! They used to put arsenic in face powder! They used to put aspartame in breath mints! Wait—they still do. And that's nuts because aspartame will kill you.

For the most part, though, businesses operate from a more civic-minded point of view. Treating everyone with respect and tolerance leads to a healthier bottom line and a cleaner corporate conscience. It also keeps you out of jail, as a variety of morally challenged yet nimble-fingered executives can attest.

However, when concern over doing the right thing turns into hypersensitivity to the possibility of in some small way maybe—just maybe—offending one person living in an abandoned mine shaft in Wyoming who may or may not write a letter of complaint . . . then you have a problem. The desire not to offend anyone has morphed with the philosophy of political correctness to, occasionally, lead businesses and businesspeople down a dark and stupid road.

We're not suggesting that we revert to the old ways of randomly offending people. The only person who can pull that off with aplomb is Howard Stern. And there's nothing random about his technique. Howard Stern's evil genius is that he offends everyone equally all the time.

We're talking about the importance of freedom, creativity, and expression. The "Don't Offend Anyone" Sacred Cow can put those righteous qualities in jeopardy. There are schools where Mark Twain's books and Shakespeare's plays aren't taught because of a fear that someone might be offended by the way they depict black people and Jews. That's crazy. That's crazier than eating aspartame. The world is a better place because of Mark Twain and William Shakespeare. To silence them because of some irrational concern of Offending Someone should be a crime.

Sometimes you need to cause offense. Sometimes you need to get in someone's face and make them think twice about what they believe. Sometimes in business, as in life, you need to stop being so damn polite and start saying what you mean.

the real thing

They no longer put cocaine in Coca-Cola. They do put pretty much everything else in there. Cherry Coke, Lemon Coke, Lime Coke, Coffee Coke, Blood Orange Coke . . . those are all actual flavors currently available somewhere around the world right now. And the person responsible for most of them is Mary Minnick. Mary was the head of marketing, strategy, and innovation for all of Coca-Cola Company. She was the person in charge of keeping the world's most famous brand . . . well . . . the world's most famous brand. She's brash, confident, and aggressive, and she's not afraid of offending people. When we describe her that way, she sounds like a really lame character from a soon-to-be canceled TV drama. But she's not. She's just a smart and successful executive who believes in being opinionated and expressive.

She started out as a lowly sales rep selling Cokes to a hot dog chain in Minneapolis. She worked her way up the corporate ladder until she got a break and joined the marketing department. One of her first products was a clear beverage called Nordic Mist. A senior Coke executive tasted it and described it as "Wolf Sweat." Ever since she started, she had a reputation for pushing hard and occasionally rubbing people the wrong way. Early on in her career, one of her managers told her, "You've pushed too hard; you've alienated everyone . . . nobody wants to work with you anymore." That's not a good internal review.

But the manager was wrong. A lot of people at Coke appreciated her intelligence, style, and aggressiveness. She was tapped to help oversee marketing in Asia. She kept scooting up the corporate ladder, and her high heels reached one of the highest rungs.

Throughout her sojourn at Coca-Cola, Mary had to battle an entrenched attitude that she found counterproductive. "There was a culture of politeness and consensus and talking around an issue, rather than taking it head-on." Everyone was so worried about doing and saying the "right thing" that no one was pushing the company forward. Interbrand estimates that the value of the Coke brand has decreased 20% since 1999. Mary found herself butting heads with a corporate-wide characteristic that was helping to feed that decline. Too much politeness and dainty tiptoeing can sap a business of the vitality that made it successful to begin with.

Mary Minnick isn't an offensive person. She has no desire to hurt anyone's feelings or alienate her coworkers. And, as far as we can tell, she hasn't. But she isn't restrained by an irrational concern that what she's about to say or do *might* offend someone. She speaks her mind and encourages others to speak theirs. If feelings get hurt, she deals with it. If someone crosses the line and is continually offensive, then that person gets fired. But someone who constantly offends others isn't a confident outspoken source of creativity and uniqueness. That person is a jerk. And, as we know from carefully studying the previous chapters of this book, there's no place for jerks at work.

the real deal

Las Vegas, however, is the perfect place for jerks. Just landing at McCarran Airport amps up your "jerk quotient." By the time you're pinwheeling on the artificially enhanced casino oxygen, you're officially on "jerk overdrive"—otherwise known as "Vegas mode." And of all the obnoxious loudmouths to be found in, on, under, and around the Strip, perhaps none is more annoying than Phil Hellmuth.

Phil is loud and whiny and insulting and condescending and dismissive and self-aggrandizing—all before breakfast! This is the man who, after being bounced out of a poker tournament, announced, "If luck weren't involved, I'd win every hand." He also suggested that a player who had just beaten him on a lucky draw "couldn't even spell poker." On another occasion he humbly suggested, "I have revolutionized the way to play Texas Hold 'Em."

What makes Phil Hellmuth such an offensive Vegas character is that, unlike 99.99% of the other offensive Vegas characters, Phil Hellmuth is an unbelievably successful gambler. He was the youngest winner of the main event of the World Series of Poker and has gone on to accumulate another ten Series bracelets since then. He has an eerie way of knowing what cards everyone else has and a preternatural talent for calculating odds in the blink of a hummingbird's eye.

If ever there was anyone who wasn't opposed to offending people, it's Phil Hellmuth. But Phil's brash style isn't just an unpleasant byproduct of spending a lot of time in Vegas. Away from the tables he is generally regarded as a smart, pleasant, fun, family guy. So why the cretinous poker personality? And why is he so successful?

The answers to those two questions are connected. Any kind of reticence or lack of confidence at the high-stakes poker table can lead to your instant demise. So, Phil doesn't limit his expressions or reactions. He refuses to be afraid of offending anyone. Also it's a stressful business and sometimes anger or relief can make you say stupid things. Early on, Phil's style got under a lot of people's skin. He quickly earned the nickname "Poker Brat."

As he got more and more successful, his reputation as a

churlish brat actually started to give him an advantage. People were eager to take him down a few pegs, so they were more inclined to make overly aggressive plays that backfired. As poker became a popular televised event, the cameras would seek out the Poker Brat because they knew he would always be inflammatory and entertaining. Seeing dollar bills everywhere he looked, Phil cultivated his boorish reputation.

These days, Phil Hellmuth is a very tall, whiny cottage industry. He makes millions at the card tables, as an author, a TV commentator, and even as a fashion designer. His clothing line is called "Poker Brat."

See? Sometimes it pays to offend people. As long as you can instantly calculate the odds of hitting the boss flush when you're up against three kings and a baby straight. We have no idea what that means, but we're sure Phil Hellmuth will explain it to us— as soon as he's done berating us for going all in with a pair of twos.

the real feel

We are simple folk with honest hearts and fresh-scrubbed faces. We help old ladies across the street, and if the opportunity ever arose, we would gladly lay our cape across a puddle so that the Queen of England could pass untrammeled. In short, we are gentlemen, and it is with great trepidation and apologies in advance that we launch into this next segment because it deals with the extremely ungentlemanly subjects of homophobia and virgins.

Don't Offend Anyone is a tried-and-true business axiom. But that doesn't mean businesses abide by it all the time. And just because we think it's a Sacred Cow and in need of immediate execution doesn't mean it's okay to offend people all the time. The merits of a particular business—like life, criminals, and extreme sports—should be tried on a case-by-case basis. Sometimes offending people is a wise way to go. Sometimes offending people is merely offensive. By way of illustration, let us segue to the eye-opening example of Snickers versus Virgin.

Snickers wanted to raise its profile by making a Super Bowl commercial that would stand out from all the others. Not content to rest on the strengths of peanuts, chocolate, and some sort of nougat, they felt they needed a little extra boost to raise their consumer profile. So, for Super Bowl forty-one (or XLI, as they like to put it), Snickers spent a bundle and aired a racy, edgy commercial that clearly wasn't afraid to Offend Anyone.

In said spot, two rough-and-tumble dudes are working on a car's engine. One of them is eating a Snickers bar. The other, overcome by desire to eat some tasty Snickers, starts eating his buddy's bar at the same time. Their lips meet and they are instantly stricken by homosexual panic. Then they hurt themselves to prove that they're "still men."

Market research indicates that initially the spot received a solid response from the public. But the geniuses at Snickers weren't content to hit the world with a quick, slightly offensive shot and then backpedal to the safety of a neutral corner. Oh, no. See, they had created a host of alternate endings for the same spot and they encouraged everyone to check out these hilarious versions on their Web site.

Well, a lot people went to that Web site and were treated to an increasingly unpleasant series of not funny but oddly violent homophobic commercials. The content was so offensive that it colored people's opinions of the original spot. In these days of instant viral Internet avalanches, Snickers was doomed even before Peyton Manning won the MVP (which he clearly didn't deserve). A massive anti-Snickers consumer campaign began immediately. Clearly, this was not what Snickers was hoping for.

Snickers wasn't afraid of Offending Anyone and ended up Offending Everyone. Virgin Atlantic, however, also wasn't afraid of Offending Anyone when they produced a recent ad for their new Upper Class service. And they also chose to mine the classically rich comedy vein of Homosexual Panic (see Aristophanes).

In this elegantly produced spot, a trim young fella cavorts romantically with a larger, hairier fella through fields and ponds and candlelit baths, all while the Bee Gees' "How Deep Is Your Love" echoes in the background. The commercial ends with the handsome guy waking up on a crowded flight to discover the obese guy sound asleep and drooling on his shoulder. Then the announcer tells us that on Virgin Atlantic's new Upper Class service, there are physical partitions between the seats to make sure that no one touches you and/or falls asleep while slobbering on your upper body.

Fundamentally, these two commercials are similar. They both play into the average heterosexual's nervousness about male-to-male intimacy. Neither spot is afraid to run the risk of offending in order to get our attention. The Virgin Atlantic people pulled back in time to prevent the offensive elements from overwhelming the piece's sense of humor. The Snickers people hurtled over the edge of offensiveness into a chasm of wasted money and tarnished brand.

Perhaps Virgin's saving grace was that, ultimately, their spot was about their product, whereas the Snickers spot was just trying to get a laugh. The Virgin ad was being teasingly offensive to highlight this wonderful new seat which offers customers privacy and comfort. There was no product-based reason for the bizarre events in the Snickers commercial to unfold. There was no defense for their offensiveness.

Just because it's not a good idea to be paralyzed by the thought of possibly Offending Someone doesn't mean it's a good idea to just go ahead and Offend Everyone. A little offense goes a long way. Too much offense and you'll be forced to be on the defensive all the time. And if you can only play defense, you'll wind up getting benched. And then you'll lose your scholarship, get drafted, and end up in a Vietnamese jungle with trench mouth and Jimi Hendrix blaring from the helicopter speakers. So, try to find the right balance between playing it safe and pushing the envelope—someday you'll thank us.

potty mouth

There are many, many clothing companies on this green, spinning marble some call Earth. Why, we can name ten different retailers currently selling the exact same striped T-shirt at prices varying from $5.95 to $88. Frankly, we can see all ten stores from our corner window here at the Sacred Cow Headquarters in the attic of New York's Chrysler building (we have a telescope). Why would someone buy an $88 version of a $6 shirt? There are two reasons: 1) Stupidity. 2) Brand cache. Frequently 1) is directly responsible for 2). And sometimes being incredibly offensive is responsible for both. Take, for example, a little outfit called French Connection.

For years the designers, marketers, seamstresses, and floor waxers at French Connection toiled away in relative obscurity. They made their little outfits, some people bought them, and life went on. Then, one day, the British headquarters of the international company received a fax from the store in Hong

Kong. The fax was sent from FCHK (French Connection Hong Kong) and addressed to FCUK (French Connection United Kingdom). After much sniggering, some bold soul decided to embrace this bawdy and nervy acronym and build an entire advertising campaign around it. (See, FCUK looks very much like a vulgar but common word in English. We can't tell you what it is, but play around with those letters and eventually you'll get there.)

Insisting that FCUK was merely an innocent acronym for their company's name, French Connection launched a massive media campaign. Their feigned innocence was never really believed since their initial T-shirt line featured slogans like, "fcuk me," "fcuk fashion," and (our personal favorite) "fcuk on the beach."

Were people offended? Um . . . yeah. The mayor of Boston forced them to remove all their public ads. When they sued another company for using a similar slogan, the presiding judge threw the case out. One of the reasons that he didn't side with French Connection was that their ad campaign was "tasteless and obnoxious."

So, you're not supposed to offend anyone, right? And French Connection offended a lot of people. So, their marketing campaign must have failed, right? Why are you asking us these silly questions? Of course it didn't fail. FCUK became hugely successful—primarily with younger buyers who respond to brashness and who are always looking for an excuse to offend people.

Suddenly it seemed like every hipster in town was parading around with some new clever "fcuk" slogan emblazoned on his or her shirt. In 2001 when the store opened in the Bay Area, they printed up a huge poster announcing that this was "San Francisco's first fcuk!" While that seems highly unlikely, no one can deny the success of French Connection's offensive advertising campaign.

In 2006 the company finally shifted gears and adopted a new campaign to convince a gullible planet to buy their stuff as opposed to someone else's. Fcuk is now a thing of the past. One of the reasons that it was replaced is that it had become so successful and so commonplace that it lost its ability to shock and offend.

Don't Offend Anyone? How about, Always Offend Everyone? We're not saying it's a viable business strategy for everyone. And it'll certainly increase your chances of getting beaten up in a parking lot. But for a glorious nine-year period it worked for French Connection. And Madonna's been doing all right with it since she was old enough to vote (which, by the way, was in 1957).

The Sales Force
Makes The Sale

Sales is another one of those business buzzwords that you can slip into any conversation if you want to sound like you know what you're talking about (but you really don't). For example, "We were in Wales with Tom Shales selling snails in pails but the gales sprang up and our **sales** failed." See? We kind of sound like Bill Gates there, don't we?

But Sales isn't just about sounding erudite and business-savvy. Sales has also birthed more Sacred Cows than a ninety-year-old Indian veterinarian. Wow. That joke was so lame we can actually hear it limping. That lame/limping joke was pretty bad too. Let's just cut our losses and get to the Sacred Cows of Sales, okay?

While there are many that we could kill for you, we will focus on just two. These are the two most commonplace Sales Cows. And what is most interesting about them is that they appear to be completely contradictory. You've heard both of these dusty aphorisms many times, but you've probably never heard them back-to-back as we're about lay them out for you. On one hand you have The Sales Force Makes The Sale. In the opposite corner lurks The Product Should Sell Itself.

The Sales Force Makes The Sale versus The Product Should Sell Itself. Two heavyweight contenders fitted out in colorful trunks ready to do battle to satisfy the bloodlust of a thirsty public.

"How can these two Sacred Cows coexist and flourish?" you ask yourself while squeezing into your ringside seat. It's a pretty good question. After all, if The Sales Force Makes The Sale, then clearly The Product isn't Selling Itself. And, conversely, if The Product Sells Itself, then why the hell do you need a Sales Force?

It's an interesting riddle—much like that thing that that guy had to figure out with that other thing in Egypt. But what's most interesting about these two seemingly opposite Sacred Cows is that they're both wrong. Unlike a title fight, this is a battle where there will be no winners. Both gladiators are going to die, and we'll be the lecherous, laurel-wreathed Caesar grinning and drooling and pointing our murderous thumbs down.

1. The Sales Force Makes The Sale

At almost every company, the Sales Force comprises a large percentage of the overall staff. This can be very helpful at league softball games as a large pool of eager and energetic go-getters yields high scores and the occasional niftily turned double play. All these Salespeople, however, also have a downside: Their sheer numbers make them inordinately powerful when it comes to generating Sacred Cows. Who do you think first came up with the idea that The Sales Force Makes The Sale? Was it Wittgenstein? Heidegger? Ruth Buzzi? No, it was some guy in Sales. Salespeople (like all people) tend to have an inflated opinion of their own worth.

Every Sales department tends to be convinced that they're the lifeblood of every company for which they work. But the Sales Force is only as good as the product they're selling. Obviously there are good salespeople and lousy salespeople. But even the greatest salesman in history would have trouble selling the wrong product to the wrong market.

The Sales Force at the Coca-Cola Company has achieved something almost unimaginable: They have made sugary brown fizzy water into the most famous item in the world. Don't get us wrong—Coke tastes lovely. But does it taste so unbelievably good that bush pygmies, Nordic cave dwellers, and old people in Florida should all love it unconditionally and equally? Probably not—but that's the case. Coke's marketing department knows how to market and their Sales Force knows how to sell.

So, in 1985, when Coke launched a brand-new product, the Sales Force was ready to Make more Sales. The only problem was that they didn't. The new product was New Coke and nobody wanted it. They were perfectly happy (nay, blissful) with Old Coke and they were not about to change. Suddenly the same Sales superstars who had been patting themselves on the back all those years looked like a bunch of slack-jawed Willy Lomans. Attention was not being paid. (Arthur Miller, wherever you are, forgive us.)

Did the Sales Force at Coke suddenly hit a wall? Or, more likely, were they only as good as the swill they were shilling?

How about the Sales geniuses at Miller Beer Company? They sure looked smart when they were selling bottles, cans, cases, and kegs left and right and hand over fist (sometimes even left hand over right fist). Then along came 1992 and Miller Clear Beer. The Sales Force spread out across the country doing their dance and singing their song. But nobody wanted to hum along and/or merengue to the tune of colorless beer. In fact, they were repulsed by it and refused to buy it.

The Sales Force at Clairol had been on a glorious run until the development department presented them with two new shampoos to hawk: Look of Buttermilk and Touch of Yogurt (we're serious, these were actual hair unguents—in bottles and everything). Not surprisingly, the general public did not respond enthusiastically to the idea of putting food on their scalps. Despite the best efforts of a once-unstoppable Sales team, nobody was buying. Once again, The Sales Force Didn't Make The Sale.

When great ideas get turned into great products, a strong Sales Force is essential. They can make the difference between never quite catching on and mega-success. But when lousy ideas get turned into lousy products, even the greatest Sales Force on Earth can't help. Your softball team may remain undefeated, but your company will get shut out.

2. The Product Should Sell Itself

While many companies have a lot of employees in the sales department, there are no companies that have employees only in the sales department. Even the sales-iest corporation in the solar system has to have at least a couple of lawyers . . . or one person in the accounting department . . . or maybe just an eight-year-old in research and development. And regardless of their lack of numbers, these non-salespeople have proven amply capable of generating plenty of Sacred Cows of their own.

The Product Should Sell Itself is clearly a Sacred Cow that was invented by someone who didn't work in sales (unless it was invented by a recently fired salesman with an axe to grind).

This hoary old chestnut has a certain undeniable appeal. It would be nice if Products Sold Themselves. It would also be nice if Products Produced Themselves, Packaged Themselves, and Deposited Large Amounts Of Money Directly Into Our Bank Accounts Themselves. Lamentably, this is not how the business world operates.

A certain amount of skepticism toward and scorn for the sales department is healthy. It's too easy to get caught up in the belief that the sales guys can sell anything. It's that kind of thinking that leads to lazy businesses and crappy products. But completely dismissing the importance of sales and marketing is a mistake as well.

As we pointed out just a few scant moments ago, the worst ideas cannot be salvaged by even the best sales teams. This, however, does not mean that the opposite is true. The best ideas can definitely be destroyed by bad sales teams. Which means that even the best ideas benefit from good sales teams. It is foolhardy to presume that whatever it is you want to sell is so essential and wonderful that everyone will buy it without being told to. Unless you have the exclusive worldwide rights to sell water or air, this kind of merchandising ubiquity is highly unlikely.

In most instances, consumers do not buy products. They buy benefits. A product is more than the sum of its parts. It needs to solve problems, create opportunities, make us feel better about ourselves and the world around us. These benefits are not usually obvious to the naked eye. Sometimes even the heavily clothed eye can't make them out. You need to explain these benefits to the consumer. You need to sell them.

Charles Revson once said, "In the factory, we make cosmetics. In the drugstore, we sell hope." This is the same man who referred to his lotions and potions as "Hope in a jar." And, before you dismiss his sayings as wimpy and not relevant to big business, he's also the dude who said, "I don't meet competition. I crush it."

Regardless of the obnoxious pomposity of many sales departments, the customer still needs to know why they should want what you're selling. They need to be told what it will do for them. They need to know how it will bring them hope. The

more persuasively you tell your story, the more likely that someone will buy it.

Revlon started out in 1932 selling one product: nail polish.
They are now a global cosmetics giant. The Revson brothers
and their partner, Charles Lachman (that's where the "l" in
Revlon comes from, by the way), didn't assume that their nail
polish was so amazingly nail polishy that it would sell itself.
They pushed and pushed hard. As the company grew and the
product line expanded, they pushed even harder.

Revlon was behind the infamous quiz show scandal of the
1950s. They were so committed to pushing their products on
the public that they manipulated the results of a live TV show to
enhance their demographics. They destroyed the lives of a
bunch of people and triggered an ongoing distrust in the verac-
ity of all television programs, but their plan worked. Revlon
emerged from the scandal as a legitimate multinational conglomerate.

Can some products sell themselves? Sure. You can move a
bunch of units of nail polish if it's really shiny and you offer it
for the right price. But how many more units could you sell if
you flex a little sales muscle? And if you align the perfect product with the ideal sales force and marketing scheme, you can
conquer the world. Let's just be grateful that Charles Revson
was content with billions of dollars, or right now we all might
be living in Glimmer Glossville riding our Colorstay to the
Frost & Glow.

Have we made our point? Or are we babbling again? Oh,
here's the nice man with our medicine. We'll be right back.

Ten Reasons Why
You Should Not Trust Us

1. We sometimes stretch the truth.
2. We don't know what we're talking about.
3. You shouldn't trust anyone.
4. Even if we're telling the truth, we could still be wrong.
5. If we were right, wouldn't smarter, more successful people have already thought of all this?
6. One of us is a convicted felon.
7. We'll say whatever we have to, to get our hands on your money.
8. No one knows more about your business than you do.
9. Your mother always told you not to trust strangers.
10. We just talked about your mother.

Ten Reasons Why
You Should Trust Us

1. Okay, we tell a few stretchers, but at least we're honest about it.
2. Hey, if we're liars and we're lying about not knowing what we're talking about then maybe we *do* know what we're talking about.
3. You trust your dentist and what has he ever done for you but cause pain and make fun of your brushing technique?
4. Even if we're lying, we could still be right.
5. Smarter, more successful people probably wouldn't waste their time trying to help you.
6. We were lying about one of us being a convicted felon.
7. Sure, we want your money, but we want to help you even more.
8. You haven't been doing such a great job with your business. Maybe it's time to let a stranger lend a hand.
9. Most of your mother's sage nuggets of advice were preceded by the sound of a bottle of Jack Daniel's being surreptitiously opened.
10. We just called your mother a drunk. You either have to trust us or fight us.

Death To All Sacred Cows

SECTION III

(carcass)

Sacred Veal *(4)*

M any of you will be happy to know that, starting in 2007, the European Union prohibited the use of movement-restricting crates and special diets designed to cause anemia in the raising of calves for veal. Perhaps some of you will be disappointed to know this. Certainly there must be a handful of old-school veal purists in small towns in central Italy who now insist that their *vitello tonnata* has been irreparably harmed forever and ever.

Our position on this matter reflects our position on most matters—we tend to see both sides. While it's true that forcing adorable baby cows to suffer through a sad, brief life of imprisonment and darkness is tragic, you can't argue with the great taste of *Schnitzel und Spätzle mit* a wedge of *zitrone* and a *wenig Spitze* of flash-fried parsley. Wash that all down with a cold glass of gewürztraminer and maybe we're leaning to the crates-and-anemia side after all.

The kind of veal to which we're referring in this chapter, however, is never dipped in eggs and bread crumbs. We're talking about Sacred Veal, which is really just the baby version of the Sacred Cow. These are newer, less engrained business thoughts which run the risk of growing into full-fledged, bothersome, stifling, constricting, industry-wide business edicts if someone (us) doesn't smother them in their sleep. Sure, we could kill them when they're awake, but then we'd run the risk of an accidental hoof in the groin and who needs that?

The Gate Strikes Back: Five Sacred Cows Of Advertising

4. *Never Reference Sex, Politics, Or Religion*

Surprising as it may seem, this is still a Sacred Cow in the advertising world. There are obvious exceptions to the "no sex" rule, but even they tend to deal with sexuality obliquely. Politics is rarely mentioned. And religion is verboten. We hate seeing the word "Never" pop up anywhere—especially in Sacred Cows and the titles of James Bond films. Our favorite recent ad is Virgin Atlantic's ten-minute promo for their new Upper Class service. The whole thing is a parody of a soft-core porn film. And the only place to see it is on the soft-core porn channel of the pay-per-view service at certain hotel chains. Sometimes flying in the face of convention and challenging the old rules is the best way to stake your claim in a new territory. And for the record, we know about the Virgin spot because of extensive Internet research. When we're at hotels, it's gym, conference room, dinner, and lights out. No matter what the accounting department says. Those incidental room charges were all just a big mistake.

E-mail Saves Time

This one probably would be a Sacred Cow by now if only e-mail had been invented sometime before whenever the hell it was invented. It sure seems like it's been around forever, doesn't it? Why, we can barely recollect the old days when the world was so very, very different. Back then, when your buddy sent you a hilarious photograph of a fat guy with his arm blubber stuck in a taxi door being dragged down Sixth Avenue, you had to photocopy it, put all the copies into different stamped, addressed envelopes, and then mail all those envelopes to all your other buddies. Now we can share that kind of wonderful hilarity with the click of a button. And that's why our civilization is going down the drain faster than Stuart Little in a tiny speedboat.

But we don't want to take unwarranted shots at today's digital culture. Let's confine our unwarranted shots to the use of e-mail in the workplace. The office e-mail universe is a place where everyone is talking but no one is listening. It has become the ultimate cover-your-butt tool.

We once had an employee who literally spent his entire day typing e-mails. Other than the occasional client meeting, he only left his office for lunch and bathroom breaks. His modus operandi was to take orders from his client via e-mail and then distribute those orders to other people also via e-mail.

His professional goal was simply to keep things moving through the system and off his desk. Now, clearly, he wasn't adding any value to his clients or our agency. But that wasn't the biggest problem.

The biggest problem was that the people to whom he was distributing these orders didn't always agree with him or understand what he wanted.

Which led to more e-mails.

Everyone was spending hours writing and reading e-mails instead of spending a few minutes talking and figuring everything out. Sometimes the e-mailers were in offices right next to each other.

This was nuts, and as soon as we identified the problem, we put a stop to it. We were going to place the offending employee in a veal crate, but we didn't want to violate EU statutes. In the interests of the prevention of animal cruelty, we just fired him.

In the old face-to-face world, we spoke our minds, had our differences, and resolved the dispute. In the brave, new e-world, we just keep responding to endless e-mail chains that date back to the very first e-mail, which was probably about how useless e-mailing is.

In the interests of not wasting more time in the pursuit of not wasting time, we established some e-mail guidelines at our office:

E-mail should be used to deliver news, not opinions.

E-mails are best when you need to tell several people the same thing.

E-mails should not take longer than twenty seconds to read.

Don't say something in an e-mail you wouldn't say in person.

Don't yell in an e-mail. Sure it's fun to use the cap key to make a point, but you'll just end up sending a bunch more e-mails to explain why you were yelling to begin with.

Since the implementation of these suggestions (and since we got rid of that goldbrick), e-mail at our office has not caused any major problems. We killed that Sacred Veal before it had the chance to grow into an unruly beast. Now all we need is the gewürztraminer. Man, that's a weird-looking word but an easy-drinking wine.

Always Know What Your Direct Reports Are Doing

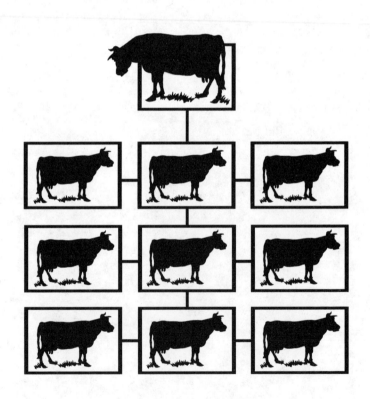

This burgeoning pain in the keister hasn't reached full Cow status yet, but it's well on its way. The idea behind it is that when you hire someone who will be working directly beneath you, it's essential that you're aware of every move that he or she makes. That's the person most closely tied to you on the corporate tether, right? If they get pulled into the metaphoric mud pit during a rousing game of company tug-of-war, then you're next. You have too much to risk to let them wander about unfettered. They could be messing up, which would reflect badly on you. Or worse, they could be plotting against you. You see how enviously they eye your glorious corner office. Keep a weather eye, friend, and Always Know What Your Direct Reports Are Doing.

Okay—you need to relax. Paranoiacs and conspiracy theorists rarely get ahead in life. Usually they end up in a disgusting mental institution with a disproportionately beautiful name—like Shady Glen or Sheltering Pines.

The people directly beneath you at work should be your closest allies and most trusted helpers. Hire them wisely. Take time to make sure that they're the best fit for the position available. And then let them do their jobs. If you micromanage them, they will resent you and probably won't do their best work. Either they'll make nervous errors and you'll get blamed, or they really will end up plotting against you. All of your misguided fears and paranoia will become self-fulfilling prophecies.

As noted horse whisperer and martial arts expert Pat Parelli has often said, "The more you use your reins, the less they'll use their brains."

Keep an eye on your Direct Reports, but don't smother them. Let them roam the grassy fields unchecked, and maybe one day they'll win you the Kentucky Derby.

Learn To Multitask

Like "e-mail" and "direct reports," "multitasking" is a relatively new introduction to the business lexicon. When we were children, we used to call "multitasking" "doing two things at once." Of course we also called the radio "the wireless," and we referred to trains as "iron horses." Nowadays, Multitasking is as hip and cool as hoola hoops and barium enemas were when we were young. My, how we miss the halcyon days of our youth when the world was an unpainted canvas, dinosaurs strolled down Fifth Avenue, and Ron Howard had a full head of hair.

Modern times, however, call for modern solutions, and in the business world, everyone is clamoring for Multitasking. It's not enough to close the deal, you also have to open the next deal and develop new markets all at the same time. Are you a brilliant graphic designer? Who cares? You also have to edit video and master AutoCAD.

But what's the point to it all? Isn't the idea behind any business endeavor to successfully complete said business endeavor? And if that's your goal, shouldn't you focus on getting that one job done as well as possible before moving on to the next?

There are times when Multitasking is beneficial. But there

are also times when Serial-Tasking is the only way to go. There will always be zany, newfangled fads like Multitasking, and Xboxing, and Totem Pole Carving. Enjoy them. Take advantage of them. But don't get so obsessed by them that you can't recognize when they're just getting in the way.

Business Should Be Serious

This bit of Sacred Veal would have been a Sacred Cow except for the fact that it was a given for so many years nobody ever felt the need to talk about it until recently. Back in the day, business was always serious. Recently, however, the marketplace has changed significantly. In the digital age there are massive industries that don't even have offices. Thousands of employees work from the comfort of their own homes where they log on to computers wearing duck slippers and Wisconsin cheese hats for all we know.

The era of the Man in the Gray Flannel Suit is a thing of the past. Somber, three-martini lunches and sensible shoes are more the exception than the rule these days. But there is a backlash against this growing freedom and openness at work. More and more people seem to be insisting that Business Should Be Serious again.

They look back fondly to the way things were and want to recapture some of those traditional qualities. Big money is at stake, after all. Careers, reputations, futures, are on the line. All of that should be taken seriously.

We have always felt that there's a difference between taking things seriously and being serious. Sometimes we have no idea what that difference is, and we have been guilty of acting like completely inappropriate morons.

But nobody thinks the people at Apple are morons. The panoply of Apple products has been so wildly successful that they have almost become the default example of postmodern business success.

So if they choose not to take Business so Seriously, we shouldn't either. Buried in the long, incomprehensible, and mind-and-eye-blurring mini-print in the legal disclaimer for the original iPod shuffle is the following warning: "Do not eat iPod shuffle."

We have no idea whether this was added intentionally or if it just slipped past a proofreader, but it made us chuckle. Why we were perusing the tiny type of the disclaimer is none of your business. Fine, we were on the toilet and there was nothing else to read. Now drop it, okay?

That bizarre aside was a weird but charming thought that got a laugh and made us feel a little closer to the company that printed it. It didn't make us doubt the efficacy of the product. It just made us feel good for a second.

So lighten up! Just because you take your business seriously doesn't mean you have to be serious all the time.

The Gate Strikes Back:
Five Sacred Cows Of Advertising

5. "Advertising doesn't manipulate society.
Society manipulates advertising."
—Carl Ally

Carl Ally is another of the gods in the pantheon of advertising. And far be it from us to take issue with anything he said. But we're going to and there's nothing he can do about it since he passed away in 1999. Society manipulates advertising. Of course this is true. But advertising absolutely has the power to manipulate society as well. It can do this to society's detriment, but it can also do this in a beneficial way. AIDS awareness campaigns have helped slow the spread of the disease in this country. Promotional spots for hybrid cars are making money for their sponsors and encouraging environmental responsibility. And crassly self-aggrandizing commercials hyping the new Microsoft operating system can encourage people to think creatively even if they don't own a computer. At the end of the day, us ad folk are in it to make a buck, but that doesn't mean we can't do some good. Why, we can envision a day when this profession will actually be considered honorable and we won't have to lie about what we do for a living. We probably still will, but it'll be nice to know we don't have to.

A Self-Indulgent Aside

There is another Sacred Cow out there that pertains directly to what we do for a living. It's perhaps not as universally recognized as the Big Boys mentioned earlier, but it's more entrenched than your average Sacred Veal. And in our line of work, it's taken as gospel: Advertising Companies Never Advertise Themselves.

Why is this the case? We have no idea. Someone's research probably showed it was an inefficient strategy. Or maybe ad agencies balk at the cost. Or maybe, deep down, they secretly believe that advertising is a fruitless waste of time and we should all be out planting trees and building houses with our hands like the Amish or Harrison Ford when he's on his ranch in Jackson Hole.

We, however, had a sneaking suspicion that Advertising Companies Never Advertise Themselves was merely one more arbitrary rule in desperate need of a few reckless fools willing to break it. And we're nothing if not desperate, foolish, and reckless.

So, we launched an ad campaign singing the praises of our ad agency, The Gate. The name of that campaign? Death To All Sacred Cows. Did it work? This ain't a cookbook you're holding in your hands, Charlie.

Cow Killing Culture

Why are some companies more successful than others at killing off Sacred Cows? Why are we asking you? We already know the answer. It's because those companies are run by people who simply don't tolerate the limitations and constrictions that Sacred Cows present. They clearly establish a corporate will to eliminate Sacred Cows, and they take steps to alter the atmosphere that allows them to flourish.

Some managers take this thought to extremes. At Sara Lee, executives wear buttons with the word "But . . ." on them surrounded by a big red circle with a red slash across it. They have outlawed the use of the word "But." This is a little nuts, but we applaud the spirit behind it. We would suggest that they also reinforce positive language by printing up encouraging buttons featuring helpful phrases like, "How about . . ." and "What if . . ."

We also acknowledge that we'd rather have burning bamboo shoots driven under our fingernails than work for a company where the executives walk around all day wearing message buttons. But everyone has their own style. The key is to find what works best for you and then run with it.

What's the best way to kill off the Cows plaguing your company and then make sure they don't return? Again—why the hell are we asking you? We have all our notes right here on the desk.

And our notes suggest that the way to achieve this is to people your business with good Cow Wranglers—employees who can spot and neutralize a Sacred Cow faster than Ricky Hyde can rope a calf.

Here are some guidelines that we use to keep our business running smoothly:

1. **Hire right:** Find smart, open-minded, thoughtful employees who are willing to speak their minds. Pay them enough to keep them happy but not so much that they think you're stupid.
2. **Reward wrangling:** Get others to see that management will not accept the status quo. Compliment Cow Wranglers in public. Occasionally buy them lunch.
3. **Out the Cows:** Call a Cow a Cow (but do not cast aspersions on the Cow's sexuality).
4. **Get rid of Cow Fanatics:** Find the people who can't let go and let them go.
5. **Proclaim that nothing is sacred:** Create an environment of questioning and healthy skepticism around the office. Don't let nobody sass you, though.
6. **Avoid personalization:** It doesn't matter if an individual working for us likes or doesn't like something. It doesn't matter if we like or don't like something. We only need to focus on whether or not the potential buyer will or won't like something.

If these six suggestions don't help, we have one further suggestion: Buy another copy of this book and read it all over again. If you still find yourself in need of guidance, keep your eyes peeled for our upcoming volumes—*Death To All Sacred*

Cows: Dating; Death To All Sacred Cows: Parenting; and *Death To All Sacred Cows: Politics.* If, after you've read everything we have to offer, you still find yourself looking for answers, well . . . at least we'll have made enough money to finally buy a new Jet Ski.

Conclusion

Books like these usually have Conclusions, so we feel obligated to tack one on as well. We can't really think of anything to Conclude, however. Obviously, in the sense of an ending, we are Concluding the book. Aside from a few ragtag pages that you might as well tear out and fold into origami swans, this sucker is finished. But in the sense of reaching an opinion about something, we don't really have any Conclusions to offer you.

Frankly, shouldn't you guys be drawing your own Conclusions from this book? We wrote the damn thing—haven't we done enough? Do you honestly expect us to synthesize all of our brilliant examples, darling anecdotes, and pointless references into one easily digestible thought nugget? That would be foolhardy. It would also require us to reread the entire manuscript, and the publisher didn't pay us enough for that.

Instead of boring you with some kind of gassy Conclusion, let us instead look to the future. In the years to come mankind will reach unheralded levels of achievement. International travel will take place in the blink of an eye. Citizens of all nations will be able to communicate with one another telepathically. Common, household toothpaste may actually whiten teeth. It's a bold, new world heading our way.

If, in some microscopic and insignificant manner, we have

helped usher in a glorious business renaissance, then . . . well . . . hooray for us. All we can do is point out the Sacred Cows, tell you why we think they deserve to die, and usher you toward our collection of knives, nunchucks, and shotguns. The rest is up to you.

But if you're doubting the existence of the kind of negative and stifling thoughts that we've been complaining about all this while, don't take our word for it. Here's a comment made by uber-businessman and all-around hotshot Steve Jobs in *Time* magazine:

> You know how you see a show car and it's really cool, and then four years later you see the production car, and it sucks? And you go, "What happened? They had it! They had it in the palm of their hands! They grabbed defeat from the jaws of victory!"
>
> What happened was, the designers come up with a really great idea. They take it to the engineers, and the engineers go, "Nah, we can't do that. That's impossible." And so it gets worse. Then they take it to the manufacturing people, and they go, "We can't build that!" And it gets a lot worse.

Steve Jobs knows something about great ideas, designers, engineers, and manufacturing people. Steve Jobs knows something about everything. Steve Jobs probably knows what color socks you're wearing right now. And what he's talking about here is the pervasive and limiting negativity of Sacred Cows.

We all have great ideas within us welling up and bubbling over like delicious, chocolaty lava cakes. But how often do we turn these great ideas into great products, services, companies, movie scripts, inventions, hair gels, or thimbles? Not that often. In our case, never as far as hair gels and thimbles are concerned (we do have a movie script if anyone is interested). Why don't we execute every great idea we have? Sometimes we're lazy. Sometimes they evaporate like Sprite on a griddle. And sometimes these wondrous ideas don't see the light of day because there are forces out there—nefarious, deleterious forces—that hold us back. These forces include Sacred Cows.

We know exactly what Steve Jobs is talking about. We've been to auto shows and boat shows and bike shows and it's true—you see the most amazing things. You can't wait for the future to arrive so you can tool around town in that experimental antigravity scooter or the SUV that runs on potato peels and happy thoughts. But when today finally turns into tomorrow, we're usually stuck with the same stuff that we were complaining about yesterday.

That's the influence of the Sacred Cow. That's tradition mixed with fear multiplied by cowardice plus some self-doubt, a few sprinkles of envy, and a dollop of clotted cream.

But sometimes tomorrow dawns and you hop out of bed to discover that someone has invented the Band-Aid overnight. Or a midsized financial services company has increased its market share by encouraging company-wide participation. Or someone's finally selling iced tea to the Chinese.

That's what happens when you kill these Sacred Cows. When you wriggle out from under their crushing weight, great things can happen. Sometimes you wriggle out from under their crushing weight, and nothing happens. Sometimes you can achieve greatness even while pinned under their massive, mottled bodies.

There are no steadfast rules that must be followed or disaster will surely strike. Conversely, breaking onerous and unfair laws doesn't guarantee that you'll achieve success. All we have to offer you is our belief in common sense, creativity, and helpful guidelines. If the guidelines get in the way of common sense and creativity, replace them with better, more effective guidelines.

Someday we'll be able to walk onto the cavernous display floor at the auto show, hop behind the wheel of the lavender-scented hovercraft made of rubies and almond bark, and float right out the door. The days of the Sacred Cow are numbered. How large or small that number is depends on all of us.

We took 3,440 in the office pool (but that was just because someone had already picked 3,439). If this book really takes off, however, that number could be reduced dramatically.

The scrumptious Doris Day once sang (in the equally scrumptious Hitchcock film *The Man Who Knew Too Much*), "*Que sera, sera*. Whatever will be, will be. The future's not ours to see. *Que sera, sera*."

Notwithstanding the fact that Doris Day was so hot in that movie that you could have fried an egg on her thighs, Doris Day was 100% wrong. We can't see the future, but we can shape it with every choice we make in the present. Blindly and dumbly accepting its inevitability while rhyming poorly pronounced Spanish words with themselves is just the kind of behavior that breeds Sacred Cows.

So rent more Hitchcock movies! Drink more eggnog! Dance to the tune played by the Nereids and wood nymphs frolicking in the fringes of your consciousness! Or don't. We don't really care. Just remember one thing and one thing only:

Death To All Sacred Cows!

Acknowledgments

This book would not have been possible without Will Schwalbe, our publisher. He saw our "DEATH TO ALL SACRED COWS" ad in the *New York Times* and told us it was more than an ad. It was a book. After we made some calls to confirm that he did, in fact, work at Hyperion and was, in fact, not a lunatic, we were sold.

His suggestions on how to judge which Cows to kill were invaluable. You, Will, are a butcher's best friend.

And speaking of people who wield sharp sticks, we'd like to thank our agent, Luke Janklow, for poking Will with his stick and getting us a more generous contract than we ever thought possible.

Next, we'd like to thank our friend, Andrew Gottlieb, for helping us translate our ideas into this 200-page manifesto. Your sense of humor made this business book funnier than any business book has a right to be.

Of course, there are a lot of other people to whom we owe a debt of gratitude, such as Philip Gregory, the CEO of The Gate Worldwide, for permitting us to write the book. And our clients and coworkers at The Gate/New York, for teaching us many of the lessons we subsequently taught in the book.

We'd also like to thank Matthew Schwab for shooting the cow on the front cover (figuratively, not literally). Plus our friends and family for telling us they'd buy copies of this book.

Yeah, we didn't believe them either.

Finally, we'd like to thank all the teachers, clients, and bosses who told us we'd never amount to anything if we didn't follow the rules. If you hadn't set such a poor example for us, we'd never have been able to fill an entire book articulating all the reasons we thought you were wrong.

Beau, David, and Bill

About the Authors

Beau Fraser

Beau never took well to being told what was what. In fact, his first spoken words were: "But . . .", "Why . . . ," "You're joking . . . right?" And "Huh?" Tired of hearing the challenging nature of these words, his great-grandmother was heard to mutter: "Tfgh jkoy schdd adphmf tsing!!!"

Alas, because she had no teeth, Beau thought she said: "That boy should go into advertising!!!" and dutifully embarked on his career.

Today, Beau is Managing Director of the New York office of The Gate Worldwide, an international marketing communications company. In addition to running the New York office, Beau sits on both the U.S. and International Board of Directors.

Prior to joining The Gate, Beau was Managing Director of Korey Kay and earlier MindFull Marketing. He also served as President of Pagano Schenck and Kay and spent his first eighteen years in the business at Saatchi & Saatchi.

While his vocabulary has increased somewhat since he was a child, the spirit behind his first spoken words lives on.

DAVID BERNSTEIN

Like most people in advertising, David originally dreamed of joining the circus. Who could blame him? There's nothing like the adrenaline rush you get from being launched out of a cannon.

Unfortunately, the circus wouldn't have him. So he turned his attentions to the only other industry whose members regularly jump through hoops: Advertising.

Today, David is the Executive Creative Director of The Gate/New York. In addition to overseeing the New York office's creative department, he sits on both the U.S. and International Board of Directors.

Prior to joining The Gate Worldwide, David worked at agencies such as BBDO, Merkley Newman Harty, Ammirati & Puris and Angotti, Thomas, Hedge.

During that time, his ads for BMW, UPS, BellSouth, and the New York Mets made regular appearances at the One Show, Clios and Art Directors Club Awards. One of his Hallmark commercials is also a part of the permanent collection of the Museum of Modern Art.

David is a graduate of Emory University and currently lives in Westchester, New York, with his wife, Peggy, and their two children, Zack and Kyra. Neither of whom has any interest in running away and joining the circus. Yet.

BILL SCHWAB

In a career as Creative Director at advertising agencies including BBDO, Fallon McElligott, Ammirati & Puris and Chiat Day, Bill has seen and killed his share of Sacred Cows.

He delighted in killing the gilded bovine in multiple new product launches, including the BMW Roadster, whose campaign, according to the *Harvard Business Review*, received "the highest recall numbers they'd seen in ten years."

Sacred Cow shootings were widely reported when he worked on successful new business pitches for United Airlines, Holiday Inn, McDonald's, *Fortune* magazine, and Charles Schwab.

Cows continued to fall as he worked for clients like GE, RCA, DaimlerChrysler, Aetna, Nikon, Reebok, and Campbell Soup, which resulted in not only a slew of creative awards but multiple Effies for outstanding marketing success.

Today he rides herd, with partners David Bernstein and Beau Fraser, at The Gate Worldwide, a $250 million London-based marketing communications firm. Their diverse client roster and offices in North America, Asia, Africa, and Europe ensures pastures that are always green, and the Sacred Cows are fat and plentiful.